D0369955

Advance Reviews

Andrew Spanyi has made a valuable contribution to the rehabilitation of business processes. He reminds his readers that because processes are nothing less than the way work gets done, they must serve as a cornerstone of substantive, lasting performance improvement. Via simple language and a workshop vignette to which all readers will be able to relate, he presents the fundamental principles of business process management and responds to the most common challenges to its desirability, viability and practicality.

—**Alan Brache**, Executive Vice President, Kepner-Tregoe, Author of *How Organizations Work: Taking a Holistic Approach to Enterprise Health* and coauthor of *Improving Performance: How to Manage the White Space on the Organization Chart*

Finally, a refreshing, engaging and articulate perspective on giving your business the competitive edge. This book provides valuable insights on the practical issues for successful enterprise-wide business process management.

—**Chris Laubitz**, Partner, The Caldwell Partners International

Spanyi's book is a very practical and easy read. I have found that moving even a high-speed Internet company from traditional functional thinking to a more customer-service driven model is indeed a challenging endeavor. My team and I have utilized the concepts outlined in the book to produced tangible results, moving our organization in new directions.

—**Serge Rochette**, Vice-President, Network Operations, Rogers Cable Inc.

A lot is being written about business process change these days. The bottom-line, however, is that any company that really succeeds at business process change does so because people care and people organize to integrate the organization around processes that are aligned with the organization's strategies. Andrew Spanyi makes the case for the people side of business process change very effectively in this short, focused book.

—**Paul Harmon**, Executive Editor, Business Process Trends newsletter (bptrends.com), Author, *Business Process Change*

Whether you are in the Board room, the management team or the front line, this is a refreshing and eminently readable work that is practical and immediately useful. It provides an approach that allows senior management to build a new thought model in their organizations for successfully implementing Business Process Management.

—**Steve Towers**, Chairman and Co-founder, The Business Process Management Group (BPMG.org)

Companion Books and Resources

When combined with the course materials associated with the book, you've got a $2,000 professional workshop in a book! This book is required reading for everyone in a process-managed enterprise.
—**Robert Boulet**, Former President and CEO
GE Capital IT Solutions Canada

The *required* and *suggested* readings referenced in this book can be obtained from Amazon and other sources at
www.anclote.com/spanyi.html

I recommend that you skim the book first, and then access the assigned reading materials for a more thorough, second read. I'd be interested in learning about your experience with the book. Email your comments and insights to me at andrew@spanyi.com
—Andrew Spanyi

Business Process Management is a Team Sport

Play it to Win!

Andrew Spanyi

Anclote Press
Tampa, Florida, USA, www.anclote.com
Providing Actionable Information for the 21st Century

Publisher's Cataloging-in-Publication Data

Spanyi, Andrew.
  Business Process Management is a Team Sport: Play it to Win! / Spanyi, Andrew.
- 1st ed.
      p. cm.
    ISBN 0-929652-02-9 (paperback)
    Includes Bibliography

    1. Management. 2. Leadership. 3. Technological innovation. 4. Executive ability.
5. Organizational Effectiveness. 6. Strategic planning. 7. Organizational change.
8. Reengineering (Management) 9. Process control I. Spanyi, Andrew. II. Title

HD58.87.S6369 2003   2003104528
658.4'063–dc21

Cover Design by **The Graphix Works (www. graphixworks.com)**
Book's Web site: **www.anclote.com/spanyi.html**
Published by
Anclote Press
310 East Fern Street — Suite G
Tampa, FL 33604 USA
Company and product names mentioned herein are the trademarks or registered trademarks of their respective owners.

Anclote Press books are available at special quantity discounts for corporate education and training use. For more information write Special Sales, Anclote Press, Suite G, 310 East Fern Street, Tampa, Florida 33604 or email sales@anclote.com

---

Anclote Press
Tampa, Florida, USA
Providing Actionable Information for the 21st Centurt

Printed in the United States of America.   SAN 249-7980
MK Printing 10 9 8 7 6 5 4 3 2

To my father, Ted Spanyi, who would have been pleased to see this book.

Table of Contents

Preface

The idea for this book was born a couple of years ago when I was struck, once again, by the fact that the existing literature on business process management did not sufficiently address the need to integrate business process thinking with strategy, organizational structure and people issues. At that time, I intended to write the book in a traditional format.

I had almost completed the first draft when I repeatedly heard several senior internal consultants and middle managers complain that when it came to enterprise business process management, their senior leaders simply didn't get it.

These people spoke with obvious emotion when they told stories of how their senior leaders appeared unable or unwilling to think systemically about the enterprise in business process terms. Instead, they claimed that their senior executives preferred to fiddle with the organization chart, and did not appear to understand the central role of *enterprise-wide* business process management in achieving sustainable performance improvement. Paradoxically, I had observed these same leaders actively support the systematic improvement of one or two key business processes.

Also, I had observed for some time that most business leaders are intensely competitive. They generally love competitive sports. So it was a bit puzzling why the take-up rate for BPM had not been more rapid and widespread, for business is indeed a highly competitive team sport. Running a business without an enterprise business process plan is analogous to preparing for a big game with only a roster of key players, no play-book and no practice.

On the other hand, I realized that the bulk of the existing literature on business process management does little to encourage widespread adoption. Unfortunately, much of what has been written on BPM is mechanistic and technical. Several of the works are long and tough to digest, and the links to strategy, organization design, people issues and technology are sometimes lost in the details.

So it's little wonder that for some leaders, business process thinking may have become to management theory what porridge is to gastronomy. Nourishing – yes, but not particularly exciting.

The more I thought about it, the more I began to suspect that if senior leaders didn't get it, it was partly because consultants and middle managers couldn't sell it. The BPM steak was clearly there, but the sizzle was fizzling out.

The ambition of this little book is to address this BIG gap. So, I then decided something more informal and conversational would better serve business leaders who are just too pressed for time to read lengthy, formal treatments of such a vital subject.

Accordingly, this book is designed to present key concepts to senior leaders in an easy-to-read, relevant and, hopefully, entertaining way. It also strives to provide guidance to both external and internal consultants who are in a position to facilitate change or advise business leaders.

The book is written such that the initial reading can be done in less than the time it takes to fly from Dallas to Boston or from Toronto to Miami. My intent is that a quick read can acquaint the reader with the essential concepts. However, my hope is that readers will then consume it more carefully a second time, and combine the book with its reading assignments to gain a more complete background and understanding of this vital subject (all the readings can be acquired through the book's Web site).

I believe that business process management is best suited to those leaders who have a burning desire to win. That's why I say it's a team sport. And the teams that count are the cross-functional teams at multiple levels throughout the organization who must deliberately and collaboratively work to create enduring value for customers and shareholders.

I am indebted to many people for the motivation to persist in writing this book. My deepest thanks go to my wife, Katalin, who has constantly provided support and encouragement.

I am profoundly grateful to Dr. Geary Rummler, who introduced me to the power of business process thinking in the nineties and whose work continues to have significant influence on my own views.

I am likewise indebted to Alan Brache who helped me several years ago to put into practice key business process concepts and more recently took time out of his busy schedule to review an earlier draft and provide valuable comments.

I'd also like to thank those business professionals and executives who were kind enough to review selected draft chapters and provide feedback; Robert Boulet, Colin Brayton, Ron Bullock, Paul Fjelsta, Chris Laubitz, Frank Lester, Susan Masterson, Pat Paladino, Rob Pearce, Michael Schoonover and Mark Towers.

—Andrew Spanyi
Hartford, Connecticut and Toronto, Ontario
June 2003

Chapter 1: Searching for Answers

Bob read the CEO's company-wide communication message for the second time. As the chief information officer at the diversified chemicals company where he worked, he understood that the situation was grim.

The message concluded with the statement, "This year's key strategic objectives are to protect margins, decrease costs, increase cash flow, and improve bottom line results." While the key priorities were clear, Bob knew that there was little consensus among his colleagues on exactly what needed to be done to deliver on these objectives.

Whatever else this meant in practical terms, this memo almost certainly meant that Bob's budget proposals for IT were going to be harder than ever to justify to the finance people. Although he had a natural ally in the chief operating officer when it came to advocating for continued investment in IT infrastructure, it was the CFO who had the most influence in the company's scorecard approach to setting strategic priorities. Bob felt that while the CFO's scorecard had reduced the amount of executive finger-pointing, it was less than balanced, tilting far more toward cost reduction that any other scorecard element.

What's more, that bit about "decreasing costs" almost certainly meant that he'd be fielding a lot of questions from division managers about projects to streamline and automate a whole variety of business activities: sales, vendor relations, regulatory, trading, finance, human resources, you name it – and each operational manager would be looking for the technological "silver bullet" they'd read about in industry magazines. This situation would certainly exacerbate the strain on his department's development resources. The pressure on his technical support budget already kept him up nights. Bob kept a picture of Chief Engineer Scott from the old "Star Trek" series tacked up over his desk; a cartoon balloon emerged from Scotty's head, reading, "I'll try to patch her together, Captain, but I need more time!"

The phone rang. He picked up and said, "This is Bob."

A cheerful voice boomed into his ear, "Hey buddy, this is Glen, how you doing?"

"Could be better," Bob said. "Let's see. The external economic environment is dismal. The price of oil and natural gas has risen dramatically – and you know what that means in our business. Our business volume is down 8 percent from last year. What else can I tell you?"

"Hey, look at the bright side. Chances are that things will get better before they get worse," Glen replied.

"I'm glad you think so." Bob said. "But just between old college roomies, I'm feeling like I'm caught between a rock and a hard place. The combination of budget constraints and the lack of consensus on the key business priorities by our executive team is a real problem. It's a huge obstacle to developing and operating our information systems."

"Look," Glen said in a softer tone, "everyone is searching for answers. Our mobile phone business is suffering too, although maybe not as much as the chemical sector. It's becoming increasingly clear to me that the old models don't work anymore. Recently, we've been spending a good chunk of time discussing what it might take to better deliver on our strategic objectives. Perhaps it's time to find a new way of looking at business. I'm even going on a three-day workshop in a couple of weeks to try and get some fresh ideas. Something you might want to consider, my friend."

"Tell me more," Bob said.

"Yeah, I'm going to attend Peter White's workshop on business process management. You may have heard of him. He was one of the pioneers of business process thinking in the early nineties. White claims that far too many organizations simply do not have a robust framework for guiding and managing the business. He believes that applying business process management or BPM on an enterprise-wide basis is part of the answer. He talks a lot about the need for organizations to get better at managing the complex, cross-departmental, technology-enabled, business processes. By the way, have you heard of him?"

"Yes, I read an article by him on organizational alignment a couple of months ago and I've heard from others that he's pretty good," Bob said.

Glen replied, "Okay, so why don't you check out the Web site. I found it informative and entertaining. It presents White's so-called eight essential principles and it's peppered with quotes from Yogi Berra. If it interests you, send him an e-mail or give him a call. He's pretty approachable. Now, let's talk about more important things. How are your lovely bride and the brats?"

After a few minutes of exchanging jibes and personal chatter, the two friends hung up. Bob smiled almost in spite of himself. Talking with Glen always lifted his spirits. He bought up White's Web site.

Bob browsed White's site quickly, but with interest. Some of White's more radical claims left him skeptical, but it looked like White had a knack for representing fairly complex concepts in simple terms without resorting to too much jargon, and White appeared to understand the major trends in technology pretty well. Bob also thought White's eight essential principles were pretty solid and the workshop overview seemed to indicate that the materials for the workshop would be well organized, providing tags to categorize the key points.

White's discussion of the "business-IT divide" from an organizational perspective was especially useful, Bob found. It helped him to see that what his firm really needed to solve was a "mental model problem" – the problem of how to come to develop a "shared understanding," as White dubbed it, that was dramatically different from the traditional functional view of the business and would allow people from different departments and with different professional backgrounds to share a common point of view on what is needed to create value for customers and shareholders, and collaborate more effectively across functional groups.

One point really caught his attention. White said that in spite of the history of reengineering and organizations' experiences with process redesign, relatively few companies could claim to have mastered the practice of managing the end-to-end, enterprise business processes that create the ultimate value delivered to customers. While each functional group or department often does a great job of managing the work processes contained inside its turf, they are less adept in the coordination of work across department boundaries – the essence of overall enterprise performance from the customer's perspective. In other words, "enterprise business processes" are those that touch more than one department, group or internal fiefdom in the company and largely determine a company's overall effectiveness.

This meant that enterprise performance, from the perspective of delivering ultimate value to customers, would be sub-optimized unless the executive team visibly led the effort to define, improve and manage these end-to-end, enterprise business processes.

Further, White stressed that IT needed to be seen as an enabler for these critical business processes. If it was not, it would be condemned to remain in the reactive posture that Bob constantly found himself in.

Bob also liked the fact that that White didn't belong to what he thought of as the "silver bullet" school of organizational thinkers – one of those people who thought that technology was going to solve organizational problems all by itself.

Now, reading over the company's priorities for the year for the third time, and anticipating the energy and time he'd be spending on the budget wars, Bob decided maybe this really was the time to get off-site for a fresh perspective. Scrolling down to the Web page he'd bookmarked, he clicked on the link to the online enrollment form and began to follow the instructions.

***

Meanwhile, White was sitting in his office, going over the enrollment for the seminar and the responses of enrollees to the pre-enrollment questionnaire he'd devised.

It was a diverse group as usual, Peter saw. That was fine with him. In fact, it was perfect. The mix of people from various functional areas and industries would lead to lively discussions, and set the stage for examining similarities and differences. After all, the message he really wanted to get across was the urgency for leaders to come to a "meeting of the minds" on what is needed to deliver on strategy and the central role of BPM in this regard. Over the course of the workshop, he was hoping that his participants would be able to accomplish that, and more.

It was something Peter felt he was in a unique position to do. He'd founded White & Co. more than a decade ago to assist organizations in achieving superior sustainable results through the application of business process thinking. He had weathered the reengineering craze of the nineties and the onslaught of Six Sigma fervor. He had grown his practice by working with a handful of thoughtful CEOs who recognized that there is no such thing as a "quick fix," and who understood White's central thesis that organizations are complex business systems, within which a change in any one component is likely to have an impact on other components.

While his practice had now evolved from business process improvement to a focus on implementing enterprise business process management for a select group of clients, Peter also ran a three-day public workshop four times a year. He joked that this was his "missionary work," but it was actually an opportunity to persuade executives from different organizations to adopt a more contemporary mental model of their organizations, based on business process thinking.

* * *

As Peter finished reviewing the list of participants, his e-mail inbox bleeped and a message from the course management system arrived, announcing a new application. He smiled. Perhaps this was the last participant he'd been waiting for to round out the group. He double-clicked the message, browsed through Bob's background information, and began to read the personal message included on the form.

"I glanced through your site," Bob had written, "and thought, finally, a business guy who gets the IT point of view! I've been aware for some time now of what's coming in the way of business process management, and some of the other topics you discuss. My problem has been communicating with the business side about the urgent need to get prepared to take strategic advantage of BPM technology when it comes, and to make a good argument to the finance folks about how investing in IT will benefit the organization as a whole."

"Of course," he continued, "I may have some tough questions about some of the things I've read. I'm interested in learning more about the claims on your Web site that BPM can play a critical role in helping organizations gain clarity on strategic direction, achieve better alignment and install more operating discipline. I like your analysis of what went wrong with reengineering, but I'm still in the "wait and see" camp about whether BPM technology will really do everything some people say it will. Still, if you don't mind me butting in from time to time, I'd be very interested in attending."

Peter smiled. He opened a new-mail message and started typing rapidly. "You're not alone, Bob. Research shows that even today, only 20 percent of companies report having tight integration between their business planning and their IT planning. That's one reason why I conduct these public workshops – to showcase the potential power of applying BPM on an enterprise-wide basis. My objective is to provide participants with a forum for discovery – an environment where people can explore the set of values, behaviors, tools and templates needed to create an organization where it is easy for the customer to do business with the company and that facilitates the efforts of employees in serving customers. It's clear to me that leaders must consciously transform the way they think about the business practices from a traditional functional style to a mental model based on business process management principles. Today, BPM is the most powerful way to leverage the organization's capabilities for optimal performance – something everyone is struggling to do in the current economy."

"As you suggest," White continued, there are some exciting new process-oriented technologies being developed. I'm personally intrigued with some of the concepts outlined in Smith and Fingar's book *Business Process Management: The Third Wave*. But a word of caution. While such technology has enormous potential, the most ominous barriers to fundamental change continue to be 'people issues.' People like you and your peers on the executive team first need to develop a shared mental model for managing the business."

"From what you've told me, I think you will find the seminar useful in this regard, and that your point of view as a senior IT manager will make a valuable contribution to the mix. I would be pleased to accept your application. You should get an e-mail shortly asking you to confirm your attendance. I've pasted below details on the required pre-workshop readings. These materials need to be read prior to attending the workshop."

Pre-workshop readings

Michael Porter, "What is Strategy?" *Harvard Business Review*, November - December 1996, pgs 61-78.

Gary Hamel, "Strategy as Revolution," *Harvard Business Review*, July-August 1996, pgs 69-82.

Robert S. Kaplan and David P. Norton, "Having Trouble with Your Strategy? Then Map It," *Harvard Business Review*, September-October 2000, pgs 167-176.

Peter read over what he'd written, found it to his liking, hit "send" and decided to call it a day. The first thing the next morning, checking the seminar's intranet site, he saw Bob's name on the list of confirmed attendees, and clicked to finalize the enrollment. "Great!" he said to himself, "We're ready to go."

Chapter 2: The Framework

Two weeks later, as Bob walked into the conference room at the Wilton Hotel, he caught sight of Glen browsing at the breakfast buffet. He walked over and they shook hands warmly.

Glen said, "Good to see you. You're looking well! I'm pleased you could come."

"You're not looking badly yourself – for an old codger," Bob replied with a smile. "Yes, this should be interesting. You know, I almost had to withdraw at the last minute. We had one of our legacy systems blow up last week and that caused all kinds of chaos. Fortunately, my people were able to restore some semblance of order, so here I am."

"Yeah, we've had something like that happen a month ago. Our CIO was pulling out the few grey hairs he had left," Glen answered. "This crisis management stuff has got to stop. Our timing for attending this session may be pretty good after all."

At that moment, Peter White approached Glen and Bob and introduced himself. They spoke briefly and then White went on to personally greet each participant.

A few minutes later White said in a clear voice, "Good morning, ladies and gentlemen. Did everybody have the chance to take advantage of the coffee and muffins at the back of the room? All right, then, if you'd be kind enough to mute your cell phones, pagers, and similar devices, we can get started in a minute or two."

"By the way, how many of you completed the pre-workshop reading assignments?"

A complete show of hands went up.

"That's a good thing," Peter exclaimed with mock severity, "else I'd have to throw you out even before getting started. Seriously folks, we really do have a lot to cover and have no time to waste."

Taking in Peter's comment in the spirit intended, the group settled into their seats around the conference table. Picking up a set of handouts from a small side table, Peter announced, "I'd like to begin with a short presentation that's summarized in the outline I'm passing around. I'll clarify some of the central notions of this workshop and describe the flow of the material we'll be covering in the next three days." "After that," he continued, "we'll go around the table to introduce ourselves, and talk a little bit about the real-life business challenges that have brought us together."

Peter hit the lights and switched on the room's projector to display a PowerPoint title slide with the White & Co. logo and the title of the workshop:

"A Meeting of the Minds: Leveraging Organizational Capability through Business Process Thinking."

"Why are so few companies beating the odds in today's business environment?" Peter began. "Why do we continue to read about the same handful of companies that consistently build shareholder value through improved performance, while many others struggle?"

"It may be in large part because most corporations are led by teams of executives each of whom come to the table with a distinct functional specialization that colors their perceptions about the strategic objectives of the organization and the means for achieving them. In a phrase, management teams often lack a *shared mental model* for leading and managing the business in a way that converts strategic objectives into effective business practices."

"The purpose of this workshop, therefore, is to provide you with a thorough understanding of how the business process management framework can be applied on an enterprise-wide basis to create organizational focus and alignment. I intend to provide you with a set of practical experiences with BPM, and some basic tools and templates, so that you can begin to plan for and implement BPM within your own organizations. By the end of this workshop, you should expect to be able to apply what we've learned to a business case in order to demonstrate your understanding of how this new kind of collaborative thought process might work. You should also have developed a personal action plan on how you will apply business process thinking in your own organization."

"The type of business process thinking required to successfully implement enterprise business process management practices is, above all, a customer-centered management philosophy that enables leaders to align their planning and operations more closely with market intelligence. This permits them to adapt more quickly to changing market conditions and fast-breaking market opportunities."

White left-clicked and the next slide came into view.

"What is business process management? I've defined it as *the deliberative, collaborative, and increasingly technology-aided definition, improvement and management of a firm's end-to-end enterprise business processes* in order to achieve three outcomes crucial to a performance-based, customer-driven firm:
- clarity on strategic direction,

- the alignment of the firm's resources, and
- increased discipline in daily operations."

"It's important that we understand that the emphasis here is on the management of a firm's end-to-end, cross-department business processes that touch customers, and not simply the improvement of specific work activities within a specific department or functional group. It's the 'white space' on the organization chart, those handoffs *between* departments, that must be managed to optimize overall company performance from the customer's perspective."

"I've observed, as have other experts in the field, that an increasing number of companies have had experience in improving or redesigning individual business tasks and activities over the past decade. Conversely, there are relatively few organizations that have demonstrated the dedication and competence in managing the entire set of *enterprise business processes* – and that is what we are here to discuss.

A clear and shared understanding of the basic definitions shown in this slide will be fundamental to the workshop."

- *Business Process* – Thomas Davenport: "A process is a specific ordering of work activities across time and place, with a beginning, an end, and clearly identified inputs and outputs: a structure for action.[1]" Note: This basic definition is easy to apply in the context of the work activities and tasks within a single department or functional group.

- *Enterprise Business Process* – the end-to-end (cross-departmental, and often, cross-company) coordination of work activities that create and deliver ultimate value to *customers*. Note: The enterprise business process spans more than one department or functional group within a company and typically reaches across trading partners in a value chain. *Coordination* stands out as the key challenge in this definition!

- *Business Process Management (BPM)* — a deliberate and collaborative approach to systematically — and systemically — managing all of a company's business processes. BPM is enabled by business process thinking and process-centric information technologies. BPM concepts apply both to end-to-end enterprise businesses processes as well as sub-processes contained within functional groups and specific departments.

"But what are the implications of thinking about the full range of business activities in terms of *business processes*? How is this different than the ways we currently think, lead and manage? What are some of the related tools and templates? What is the role of enabling technology in this respect? These are topics we'll explore in depth over the course of this workshop."

"As this next slide illustrates, the workshop agenda is structured along practical lines. This morning we will cover the BPM framework. Here you will see that BPM requires that the executive team think, lead and manage differently and more systemically about their business."

"This afternoon we will discuss what I call 'strategic focus.' In this segment we will explore how BPM can assist leaders to develop greater clarity on strategic direction and cascade it throughout the organization."

"Tomorrow morning, we will consider what's needed for what I call 'organizational alignment.' This involves making fundamental decisions to better align an organization's resources to achieve key business priorities. This outcome is achieved by a gaining a deeper appreciation of the interdependencies between business process performance, organization design, measures and rewards."

"Tomorrow afternoon, we will look at how BPM practices can serve to reinforce what I call 'operating discipline.' This involves tightly integrating business process thinking with operating practices and business leaders' roles in sustaining focus and alignment."

"Along the way, I'll introduce, and we'll discuss, what I consider to be the eight essential principles of business process management. They are listed in your handouts and you should keep them handy for reference throughout the workshop."

1. Look at the business from the *outside-in,* from the customer's perspective, as well as from the *inside-out.*
2. Tightly integrate strategy with enterprise business processes.
3. Articulate strategy to inspire, from the boardroom to the lunchroom.
4. Design enterprise business processes to deliver on strategic goals.
5. Ensure that organization design enables enterprise business process execution.
6. Deploy enabling technology based on the value added to enterprise business process performance.
7. Hard wire the enterprise performance measurement system to budgets and operating reviews.
8. Sustain focus and alignment.

"We'll also consider some of the major pitfalls and opportunities related to implementing these essential principles. While there will be a number of exercises throughout the workshop, on the final day, we will work on a case study to consolidate our thinking."

***

"Now, given this brief overview, let's take a few minutes for personal introductions. In addition to the typical information on yourselves, please share with us your expectations or areas of interest for this workshop. Perhaps you'd be kind enough to kick things off, Bob, and then we can just go around the table."

"My name is Bob Lockard; I'm the CIO for a major, diversified chemical company. We have had a number of challenges in connecting our IT planning to business planning. So, one of my key interests is to learn how BPM methods can bridge the business-IT divide."

"Looks like I'm next," Jim said. "I'm Jim Anson. I'm the VP and CFO for a regional high-speed cable Internet service provider. I expect to better understand how BPM can improve our ability to measure performance and thereby better manage the business."

"I'm Glen Forth, VP of network operations for a regional wireless phone service provider, and I'd like to see how BPM can assist in more effectively lining up our company's resources with strategic direction, especially when it comes to getting better payback on investments in deploying network technology."

"I'm Dave Thomson, VP of manufacturing for a national custom equipment manufacturer, and I'm principally interested in how BPM can help a company to get better clarity on strategic direction, but I share Jim's interest in measurement as well."

"I'm Lori Phillips, sales director with a pharmaceutical company. I want to understand the key steps in implementing BPM. I'm also curious whether BPM can be put into practice from the bottom-up."

When Peter had finished writing Lori's expectation on the flip chart, he turned to her and asked, "Just for clarity, could you say more about your curiosity in implementing BPM from the bottom up?"

"Sure," Lori said. "What I mean is, could I implement BPM in my department and gradually influence the rest of the company to come on board?"

Peter said, "Thanks, that's what I suspected you meant. To date, my experience has been that enterprise BPM needs to be implemented from the top down, for it's the resolution of cross-departmental issues that offers the greatest payback in terms of overall company performance. The executive team has the ultimate accountability for strategy that drives enterprise business process definition, which in turn drives the framework for performance measurement, organization design and operating practices. On the other hand process innovations often come from the bottom up, from front-line workers, especially those that interact directly with customers. Given your stated interest, Lori, maybe you could raise questions on 'bottom-up' issues periodically throughout the workshop?"

Lori smiled wryly and nodded.

"I'm Fred West, VP of marketing for a railcar manufacturing and leasing company. Just sign me up for what's been said so far."

"I'm Harry Bronson, VP of parts for a national agricultural equipment manufacturer. In addition to what's been mentioned, I'd like to learn how BPM can fit into our Six Sigma initiatives."

"I'm Robin Lima, VP of commercial lending with a regional bank, and while I think the others have covered most of my areas of interest, I'd be interested in better understanding how BPM can help us become more customer-centric."

Peter finished writing the list of expectations on the flipchart. He turned to the group and said, "Thank you, that's a pretty solid list. We'll revisit the list at the end of our workshop and see to what extent it will have been satisfied."

"As for my expectations, I hope to influence your thinking such that you leave this workshop with the knowledge and skills you need to view and lead your company's business more systemically."

"This workshop involves some pretty hard work. There will be reading assignments both tonight and tomorrow night. I'll be encouraging you to work quickly. Along the way, I'm also hoping we'll have some fun," Peter continued with a trace of a smile. "As you've probably seen on my Web site, I'm a fan of the great baseball player, coach and philosopher Yogi Berra, so, please be ready for the odd Yogism."

***

"Now, let's get into the BPM framework."

"In the introduction to their 1991 book *Improving Performance – How to Manage the White Space on the Organization Chart*, Dr. Geary Rummler and Alan Brache warned readers of the risk inherent in adopting piecemeal approaches to managing change and managing their business. In hindsight, it's unfortunate that most companies did not heed this warning over the past decade."

"We have seen that organizations have a tendency to implement various management disciplines in a manner that resembles the behavior of individuals at a Chinese buffet, where each person picks and chooses their favorite items."

"CEOs, consultants, and academics alike expound on the need for firms to adopt a common framework for viewing the business, which stimulates the firm's ability to adapt and creates the means to translate plans into results."

"Over the next three days, we will explore how BPM can help you do just that."

"Again, I define BPM as the deliberative, collaborative, and increasingly technology-aided definition, improvement and management of a firm's enterprise business processes. Although BPM can apply to departmental-level business processes, the vital challenge is enterprise business process management. For example, a company may have a fully optimized, world-class internal payroll process, but go out of business if its enterprise business processes fail to deliver compelling value to its customers. Shucks, what company would even need a payroll process at that point?"

"Also, if you've read any of my recent writing on the subject, you know that I believe that the technology to enable BPM is maturing fast, and that businesses need to prepare the way for BPM systems or risk losing competitive advantage."

"On the other hand, I don't think anyone in this room believes any longer in the kind of technological 'silver bullets' that management consultants were promising us a few years ago, –and some are still promising."

A few rueful chuckles were heard around the table.

"Based on your reaction to what I just said, I suspect that some of you know exactly what I mean. While new technologies may soon enable us to manage and operate our businesses in radically new ways, they do not and will not provide a substitute for executive decision making. To take full advantage of BPM technology, we need to radically rethink our approach to how we lead and how we manage work within our organizations," Peter continued. "That's also why we're here this week to talk in depth about the human and organizational factors implicit in BPM."

"Take the Yogism that baseball is 90% mental, and the other half is physical. That might well apply to business in general and the practice of business management. After all, *business is a team sport*, and as we'll see, it's the attitude and the work of cross-functional teams at multiple levels throughout the organization that really counts when it comes to getting results."

White's analogy got more than a few smiles.

"Let's start by summarizing what I believe are some basic environmental assumptions that reinforce the need to find new ways of leading and managing an enterprise. We are living in an age where there is more *change* than ever before and the rate of change is gathering speed. If anyone doubts that, I encourage you to scan Jim Harris' recent book, *Blindsided*. It's on your references list. Not only will we continue to see a rapid pace of change, especially in technology, but *customer power* will likely continue to increase, and competition will remain fierce in most sectors."

"Now, let me briefly cite some of the assumptions underlying the management practices I believe are implied by the business process management model."

"Business process thinking is predicated upon the central belief that it is fundamentally the complex, cross-departmental, technology-enabled, business processes that create value for customers and shareholders. Let me say that again, *"Business process thinking is predicated upon the central belief that it is fundamentally the complex, cross-departmental, technology-enabled, business processes that create value for customers and shareholders."*

"This predication assumes that every significant management activity should begin with an analysis of customers' needs and have, as an intrinsic objective, the shared understanding of the key business processes or organizational capabilities that are critical to satisfying those needs."

"This perspective is necessary in order to enhance an organization's ability to adapt, based on fast-breaking market challenges and opportunities, and to reduce the amount of time and effort required to plan and implement operating changes."

"A related key assumption is that *strategy begins with the customer.* Organizations must be designed, led and managed in a way that makes it easy for the customer to do business with the company. This business model requires a clear statement of strategic direction, based on actionable business intelligence about the customer and the market. By definition, this way of thinking about strategy involves difficult choices about the allocation of resources."

"This belief in customer-centric strategy is also reflected the methods that an organization uses to set and communicate strategy internally. It presupposes an environment that supports the efforts of employees to serve customers. It's manifested, not only in the organization's customer-facing policies, but also in its structure, its internal channels of communication, its system of rewards and incentives and its business culture."

"Another key assumption of the business process management model is that organizations are complex business and social *systems* in which a change occurring in one component is likely to affect other components. In order to achieve and maintain strategic focus, companies must plan for and facilitate customer-driven change from a point of view that transcends organizational boundaries. The extent to which this model is embraced by an organization is evidenced by the degree to which it incorporates cross-functional and cross-company communications and planning practices, and by the degree to which it demands, and rewards, cross-group collaboratioffOne factor that differentiates BPM from other management systems for evaluating and managing performance is its conceptual framework and the promise of its enabling technology. The most important features of this framework are, first, the explicit definition of business processes, including the key inputs, steps, and outputs; and second, the recognition of critical interdependencies and clarity around the fact that cross-functional collaboration is how organizations truly create value for customers and shareholders."

"This way of thinking is dramatically different from the traditional functional way of thinking that has dominated the mindset of the leadership team in many organizations. Departmental silos and turf protection that impede performance are the natural enemies of business process thinking and BPM."

"Let's also understand that BPM assumes that enabling technology is *a necessary but not a sufficient* condition for success. Major software companies are placing BPM front and center in their offerings. This new wave of process-centric technology is maturing to the point where, for the first time ever, companies will soon be able to rapidly and inexpensively model and implement process automation to power business processes performance and measurement."

"But wait. There is indeed a catch."

"As part of the dot-com phenomena of the roaring nineties, many, many companies rushed out to buy multi-million dollar customer relationship management (CRM) systems, fearing they'd be left behind if they didn't. Today, there are stories in the business press about the utter failure of such systems. Why? Customer relationship management is about work processes, not a software package. The lesson learned is clear. If companies don't *first* instill *business process thinking* throughout the organization, from top to bottom, BPM systems and technologies are simply going to fail – full stop. Technology alone will not create the kind of collaborative human relationships needed to make BPM work. To adopt collaborative working methods requires *leadership* by senior managers who are held to account and rewarded for the performance delivered by the cross-functional processes they oversee."

"Let's turn to the first two essential principles of business process management, listed in your handouts."

"First, look at the business from the outside-in, from the customer's perspective, as well as from the inside-out. This principle requires that we understand what customers expect in terms of the products or services provided, and how we are doing in providing those products or services. Let me now outline the basic steps in setting up the enterprise management framework needed to satisfy this principle."

"It's necessary to *explicitly define* customer requirements. Then, the next step is to *explicitly define,* on an enterprise-wide basis, the critical business processes that will create the value demanded by customers – and, therefore, provide shareholders with solid returns. The explicit definition of the enterprise business processes requires that for each major business process we have clarity around the inputs, key sub-steps, functions involved, outputs and key measures."

Second, in order to tightly link business strategy to enterprise business processes, it's important to measure the current performance of each critical business process in relation to customer requirements. This equips us to *express the organization's strategy in business process terms,* in part by determining the desired level of performance, and then using specific criteria to assess the gap between current and desired performance – or in business redesign terms, as-is and to-be."

"The executive team needs to act both deliberately and collaboratively to express strategy in terms of business process performance, requiring agreement on who will assume ownership of key business processes. Once 'process owners' are appointed, they will direct the execution of a limited number of critical initiatives and manage the performance of the full set of enterprise business processes."

"The BPM framework provides the means to rationalize an organization's strategic focus by objectively describing the degree of improvement needed for company-critical business processes. The BPM framework provides leaders with the means to articulate a firm's strategic direction in a meaningful and potentially inspiring way. It creates a context for decision-making in the areas of organizational alignment, including both business process and organization design, encompassing the needed metrics and rewards. Further, the framework creates the right perspective for augmenting the degree of discipline related to measuring progress toward strategic goals."

Peter switched the main lights back on, "Any questions on what I've said so far?"

There was brief silence as everyone finished scribbling notes.

Robin, the commercial lending vice president, said, "I'm not sure what you mean by 'explicitly defining' customer requirements. At our bank, we do regular customer satisfaction surveys. We ask our corporate clients to give us feedback on the degree of satisfaction with our relationship management and the specific financial services we offer. Is that it?"

Peter said, "Well, that's part of it. Surveys of customer satisfaction are useful. But there's more to explicitly defining customer requirements. It begins with clear measures of exactly what customers expect in terms of the quality and timeliness of your products and services, and goes on to express how well you are doing in providing them. In your business, for example, let's consider corporate loans. Ask yourself the following questions. Do you have specific information on what customers expect with respect to the turn-around time, terms and conditions for loan approval?

What about customer expectations on loan administration? From an internal perspective, do you have specific data on cycle time for loan approval or variance to promise date? Is there a system in place to measure the average cost for approving and administering a corporate loan? These are just some of the questions to ask and answer to explicitly define performance. Does that help?"

Robin replied, "Thanks. That makes more sense to me now."

Fred, the marketing vice president from the railcar company, then said, "I was struck by what you said about turf protection. What are some of the other obstacles to business process thinking?"

"We'll cover several other obstacles over the next three days," Peter replied. "For now, let me just briefly mention a couple of the big ones. In addition to the very real obstacle represented by traditional functional thinking, I've observed there is often a reluctance to modify management reward systems to support business process performance. I'm puzzled and frustrated by this when I see it happen. It's as if some leaders assume that they can go on rewarding the same old thing, and yet, expect different results."

"The other big obstacle I observe is around the deployment of information systems. BPM depends on enabling technology. But too often, the deployment of technology is more disabling than enabling. This happens when the focus is more on technology architecture and applications than on business results, which, in turn, means business process optimization. For example, the people at a company I worked with last year had such an adversarial relationship with their IT department that they had some very unflattering names for them, only used behind their backs, of course. That's not what I would call a collaborative environment."

"We'll talk more about these obstacles and others over the next couple of days."

Dave, the manufacturing executive, said, "In our firm, we've been talking a lot about organizational capabilities. How does the BPM framework help define and improve key capabilities?"

"That's a terrific question, Dave," Peter replied. "Management literature is pretty fuzzy around the exact meaning of terms such as 'capabilities.' I believe that what people often refer to as capabilities is simply the outputs or descriptors around business processes or sub-processes. Think about it. Companies talk about capabilities like 'first to market,' 'perfect orders,' 'lean manufacturing' and 'flawless service delivery.' The BPM framework not only leads to clarity on what business processes need to perform at which levels to improve these capabilities, but it also highlights the significant linkages between and across key business processes."

"Well," said Jim, the Internet service provider's CFO, "there's certainly a lot to think about there. If I'm not getting ahead of the game, though, I'd like to ask, what are the major differences between the model you've outlined here and an approach like, let's say, the balanced scorecard?"

"We'll certainly get into that more deeply in the next few days," Peter replied. "But I'm glad you brought it up, especially since it ties into one of the reading assignments. The short answer is this. There's a lot to be said for the balanced scorecard methodology, especially as articulated by Kaplan and Norton in their book, *The Strategy-Focused Organization.* I like what they say around translating strategy into operating terms, making strategy everyone's daily job, and working to make strategy a continuous process. The evolution of the balanced scorecard concept has elements designed to monitor an organization's progress toward strategic goals."

"So does BPM."

"The balanced scorecard approach, however, does not explicitly establish the connection between business process performance and customer requirements, Jim. In fact, the balanced scorecard design of distinct quadrants may sometimes do more to separate than to link."

"Business leaders can deploy BPM to make this vital connection."

"Furthermore, while BPM has a clear business process predisposition, the balanced scorecard has a potential functional bias that can be problematic. Particularly troublesome is what I see as an insufficient treatment of business processes in the alignment of the organization to strategy. We'll explore that in our session on organizational alignment later, and we'll see that integrating the balanced scorecard within BPM can be a very powerful combination."

"I found myself with similar questions," said Harry, the parts division vice president. "Nothing you've said so far really sounds *that* different. We used to do process mapping and 'concept to customer' spaghetti charts, for example."

"But now the executive suite is saying we've got to be more aggressive, turn things around faster, and be more 'agile' – whatever that means. Process mapping *is* a pretty time-consuming process. Sometimes too many cooks spoil the broth, if you know what I mean, and sometimes you can't see the forest for the trees. How does BPM differ? What are the practical tools?"

"You've put your finger on what I think is a significant drawback that's common to a number of the 'process mapping' approaches that superficially resemble what I'm talking about here," Peter said.

"We'll be looking critically at some of those tools, but let me put it this way for now. A key challenge for many organizations is to deal with the level of detail in business process thinking. We are not talking about spaghetti charts or about brown paper maps that cover all the walls in the executive boardroom. That kind of mapping of processes is often *linear* rather than *cross-functional*. But even when it *is* cross-functional, it's not the same thing as the business process management approach unless it's *tightly integrated with strategy* and concisely pinpoints the critical business processes to identify which processes must be improved for the firm to deliver on its strategic goals."

"The BPM approach begins with a high-level schematic or chart that describes a company's major business processes in terms of its inputs, key steps, outputs and the functions involved. This does not imply linear input-process-output chains of work activities and tasks, for the work of functional departments occurs in parallel with each department working on its own time clock. *Coordination of such parallel work activities* is a core concept of BPM. The focus is less on graphics and pretty charts, and more on achieving a shared understanding of the linkages and required performance levels by the executive team. That's why my definition of BPM emphasizes that it is 'deliberate' and 'collaborative.' Does that answer your question Harry?"

"Yes … in part. But I'll be looking forward to seeing the tools," Harry said.

Glen, the network operations vice president, said, "I have a two-part question. First of all, process thinking has been around for over a decade. Why haven't these practices been more widely adopted up to now? Next, what has changed? Why is this model the right one – today?"

"Thanks, Glen. I was wondering when someone would ask that," Peter said. "Yes, business process thinking has been around for awhile. As you know, process thinking was *implicit* in much of the quality work of the seventies and eighties, and was treated explicitly in the articles and books published by Thomas Davenport, Michael Hammer, Rummler and Brache and others, in the nineties."

"But the nineties witnessed two significant detours from the path of process management. The first was the disappointing way in which reengineering was approached by many organizations. It became essentially a search for the 'killer app,' the 'silver bullet.' More emphasis was placed on 'blowing up' current practices than on the continuous improvement and ongoing management of critical business processes. For many, reengineering became synonymous with cost-cutting and *downsizing*. It did little to transform the functional mindset of executives, and in some cases, actually reinforced command-and-control practices."

"The other detour had to do with a key challenge in the area of process measurement, one of the cornerstones of BPM. In the early nineties, when executives asked whether their IT systems could routinely measure the timeliness and quality of customer-touching business process performance, they got the answer you hear in the popular TV commercial for Hertz Rent-a-Car – *Not exactly.*"

"Then enterprise-wide information systems called enterprise resource planning or ERP systems came on the scene with outsized promises of unprecedented flexibility and robustness in IT systems that could implement and integrate business processes. Many companies realized too late that the ERP systems that seemed malleable during the design phase proved to be *inflexible* once implemented – *cast-in-concrete* might be the better term."

"So, to your second question, Fred, what has changed?"

"Many executives have developed a deeper understanding of the difference between reengineering and BPM, and current advances in technology offer new hope. Some IT experts believe that the capability already exists to automate what business process advocates have been asking for over a decade. There is increasing evidence that we will soon see the automated capability to *manage* the dynamics and complexity inherent in business processes. This is something very new, and much needed to cope with the dual forces of globalization and commoditization, which demand communication among cross-company systems, and is driving the inevitable adoption of BPM."

"In spite of the fact that it's very hard work and makes some executives very uncomfortable, the business process way of thinking hasn't disappeared. Indeed, the time has come for a renaissance in business process thinking and the IT systems needed to transform thinking into doing."

"The good news is that there's a groundswell building, in both the academic and business communities, as people who were originally drawn to business process thinking years ago refresh their level of knowledge and degree of interest."

"During the past couple of years we have seen a resurgence in the promotion of business process thinking and BPM, including work by last decade's process pioneers, such as Dr. Michael Hammer's *The Agenda* and Alan Brache's *How Organizations Work*, as well as emerging thought leaders, such as Howard Smith and Peter Fingar with their groundbreaking book, *Business Process Management: The Third Wave.*"

"New Web sites on business process management such as bpmg.org, bpmi.org, bpm3.com, www.manyworlds.com and bptrends.com have been established to promote business process principles."

"So, on to your third question. Why now?" Peter asked.

"It could well be that process thinking and BPM is nearing what Malcolm Gladwell calls the 'tipping point,' the title of his best-selling book, published in 2000. The simple elegance of business process thinking makes it both effective and memorable. Indeed, I believe it was Albert Einstein who said that everything should be made as simple as possible – but not simpler. So yes, I think the stage is set for BPM to take its rightful place in the boardrooms of the nation. This has been a long answer to a short question, but in my opinion, the key question is not 'if' – but 'when' will leaders have the vision, courage and determination to take full advantage of business process thinking?"

The room was silent.

"If there are no further questions for the moment, I'd suggest we take a fifteen minute break," Peter said. "For those of you new to the hotel, the restrooms are about 30 yards down the hall to your left. Thanks, and let's reconvene in fifteen minutes."

***

Glen, the network operations vice president, walked back into the room and went over to get some more coffee, where Jim, the CFO, was also getting a refill. Turning to Jim, Glen said "Well, what do you think so far?"

"So far, it's okay," Jim replied. "But the bean-counter in me is concerned with how much process thinking may cost to actually implement. We've had our fair share of consultants coming to us with the latest and greatest. It gets a little tiresome after a while."

"Yes, I know what you mean" Glen replied. "By the way, I was interested in your question on balanced scorecards. Is that what you use in your company?"

Jim nodded.

"How's it working for you?"

"Our public position is that it's great," Jim said. "But, privately I know that there are some issues. Some managers regard the scorecard effort as something the finance guys want us to fill in. We've had some difficulty in engaging the front line troops. They think it's too complicated. I don't know, maybe it is. Maybe we've made it that way."

"Yes. It's tough to get everyone on the same page. I've struggled with that in our Network Operations group. Even though I take care to express our goals clearly, I sometimes get feedback that it's just top-down rhetoric," Glen said. "Oops, looks like Peter's ready to get back to work."

Chapter 3: Strategic Clarity

When Peter re-entered the room, people began to drift in from the hall, pocketing their cell phones, and broke out of the small clumps of conversation scattered around the room. "Okay," Peter said when the participants had settled down. "For the balance of the morning, I'd like say a few words to conclude my overview of BPM and then introduce this afternoon's topic, strategic focus."

"What do most companies want? In a word, they want results. This means increased revenues and higher earnings. But while you can target improved results, you can't *manage* results. You can only manage the clusters of activities, often called *business processes*, and sometimes dubbed *capabilities*, that are most likely to produce the desired results. That's why implementing BPM practices throughout the organization is the best method by which organizations can produce the desired results."

"Now, you'll recall my conviction that there are eight essential principles that need to be respected in implementing BPM. Earlier, I introduced the first two of these."

"Both of these depend upon a customer-centric view of business and the explicit definition of customer requirements and strategy tightly linked to the enterprise business processes that serve customers' needs. Both principles are especially critical to achieving strategic focus. I can't stress enough that strategy must begin with the customer."

"I also believe in the concept, originally outlined by Michael Porter in his 1996 article, "What is Strategy?" that competitive advantage is about *being different* in such a way that competitors would face many obstacles in copying success. Strategic focus begins with this combination of focus on the customer and the convergence of executive thinking on what it takes to differentiate the firm and its offerings."

"To further illustrate the mindset required for the first principle, let's consider a simple example, first from a customer's point of view and then from the company's point of view. Let's say that that I want to order some office supplies. From the customer's point of view, what might the customer want?"

"Well," Robin said, after a brief silence, "I guess I know what *I* would want. I'd want the company to have what I want, when I want it, and I want good value. I don't want ordering and payment to be a hassle. I want the stuff to get here on time without me having to waste time checking up on the order. And I hate having to send stuff back because it's damaged or it's not what I ordered."

"Right," Peter said. "You want value for money, range of choice, ease of ordering, no backorders, ease of payment and reliable delivery. That just about covers the bases."

"Now consider the company's point of view. Certainly, the company would want to measure and manage the extent to which their business practices are working to provide what customers want: on-time, complete and quality products. They would want to assure ease of ordering and the payment would need to include the option to pay and order by phone or over the Internet, as well as accurate credit and invoicing services. They would also want to measure and manage the flow of activities across departments. For example, reliable delivery would mean fast, effective coordination between order takers and shipping staff."

"That's a very brief and simple illustration of looking at the business from the outside-in and the inside-out. If the company can see the business from a customer's point of view as well as an internal perspective, it's better positioned to do an effective job at managing its promotion program, its order-taking, its pick, pack and ship practices, its inventory replenishment practices, and its billing and collection, and it has a better chance of both defining and achieving targeted business results."

"Now let's talk about your lines of business. What do your customers need and demand?"

Glen, the network operations executive, spoke up first this time, "In the wireless industry, we believe that customers demand variety, value for money, hassle-free activation, reliable service, ease of payment, and ready access to knowledgeable customer support."

"That's clear and concise!" Peter said. Now, ask yourself the following questions: Does your leadership team, at least, have a shared understanding of customer needs? Do you really know what is meant by 'variety' and 'value for money'? Is there comparative data available on how 'hassle-free' your company's activation performance is, relative to others in the industry? Have you defined the major customer-touching business processes and assessed how these are performing in meeting customer requirements? How are you doing relative to your competition with respect to 'reliable service' as measured by 'dropped calls' and 'no signal' reports? What percent of your customers are paying by Internet banking, pre-authorized payment or credit card? How do these percentages compare to the industry? Do you have a mechanism to survey the environment, in order to identify bleeding-edge technology and rapidly decide the position your company will take in commercializing such technology? These and other similar questions will tell you the extent to which you have the mental model of looking at the business from the outside-in and the inside-out."

Glen was smiling as he wrote a few notes, and he wasn't alone.

"Okay," Peter continued, "the next point is this. It's virtually impossible to manage activities that are neither documented nor measured. This is true at the task level and equally true for enterprises. So, let's take a look at one business process schematic that facilitates a customer-centric view and helps to illustrate the framework for an organization to gain clarity on strategic direction and manage the business practices that really count."

Bringing up a PowerPoint slide, Peter continued, "To build on our office supplies example, this diagram outlines the customer requirements and major business processes of a Regional Office Supplies and Equipment Company, actually a company I worked with some time ago, which we'll call ROSECO. Naturally, I've modified some of the data to protect client confidentiality."

"As you can see, this company is organized along traditional functional lines: sales, marketing, retail operations, consulting services, finance, purchasing, information technology and human resources. The schematic shows the major cross-departmental business processes in the enterprise and the services delivered to customers. It also shows the key points of contact with customers. This simplified chart format was adapted from the approach outlined by

Rummler and Brache in their book, *Improving Performance: How to Manage the White Space on the Organization Chart.*"

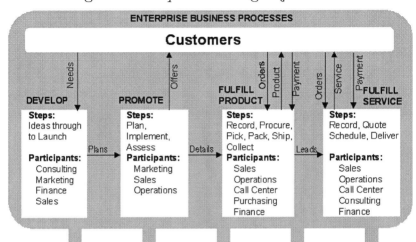

ROSECO's Enterprise Business Processes (simplified)

"How might the executive team employ this diagram?"

Jim, the CFO, was quick to respond, "I can see several potential uses. They could overlay the key performance measures on the major business processes. It would also help in the selection of process owners. They could even use it to develop service level agreements between internal departments to define needed performance levels."

"Yes. Your first two applications are right on the money," Peter said. "With respect to the point on service level agreements, you would probably need to dive into a more granular level of detail on the cross-departmental handoffs. Anyone else?"

Bob, the CIO, said, "I can see how it might provide the framework for discussion around the deployment of enabling technology for activities like order-taking, shipping, customer relationship management, just-in-time stock replenishment and so on."

Peter said, "Yes, that's true at a high level."

Robin added, "It might be the starting point to identify opportunities for improvement."

"Definitely," Peter replied. "However, to do that, we would have to overlay more specific information on performance gaps and issues. As we'll soon see, this is quite easy to do."

"Now, I have a question for you. How many of you have a similar diagram or chart for your own firm at the enterprise level?"

After a brief silence, Fred, the marketing executive, said, "We have a map for the sales process, but I suppose we're missing the big picture at the enterprise level."

"We're in the same boat, Bob added. "We've got the supply chain process nailed, but don't have clarity on the linkages to the other key business processes or the measures for these business processes from a customer's view."

"Actually, that's fairly common," Peter replied. "Most companies have an organization chart that outlines the structure of the firm and the reporting relationships. Many have even documented one or two critical business processes. Very few, however, have a graphic representation that captures the flow of work in terms of the major enterprise-wide, cross-functional business processes, providing a template for discussion of performance and dependencies."

"Maybe I'm missing something," Lori interjected. "It just seems to me that ROSECO has a pretty simple business model. Our pharmaceutical business is much more complex. We need to deal with government regulation and insurance companies. Also, while we detail prescription drugs to physicians, the end customer actually buys from the pharmacy. I'm concerned that our business is just too complicated to represent all the business processes graphically on the enterprise level."

"Yes, it's true that some businesses are more complex than others," Peter replied. "Just ask yourself, *who made it that way?* What's the benefit of having a business so complex that when one tries to depict who is accountable for business process performance, the answer appears to be that it's no one and everyone?"

"However, I've yet to see a business where we can't concisely document the enterprise view. The challenge has to do with managing the detail at multiple and increasingly lower levels. This can be accomplished by layering and leveling. That is, high-level enterprise business processes can be broken down into lower levels where more and more details are described at each lower level. Many departments already have umpteen detailed work activities documented in great detail, but it's the high-level, enterprise business processes that are too often neglected as they cross departmental boundaries, and no one has been made explicitly responsible for them."

"If you can describe the business in terms of the key enterprise business processes in a hundred words or less, you can develop the enterprise business view. If you're willing, Lori, we can test that right now. Would you take a minute or two to describe your business in terms of the big blocks of activity?"

"All right," Lori said. "Well, in the pharmaceutical business it all starts with research. Then, when we discover a viable new formulation, we go into development including clinical trials. If all goes well, we seek regulatory approval and lobby the insurance companies to offer coverage and promote the drug based on factors such as safety, efficacy and cost. In the meantime, we are running the business by managing relationships with physicians and pharmacists, promoting our brands and our company, producing compliant products, taking and fulfilling pharmacists' orders and carrying out patient education. All this needs solid procurement, enabling technology, and other supporting services like financial reports, legal and human resources. Whew, did I make it in less than a hundred words?"

"You were pretty close," Peter said with a chuckle. "So depending on how finely you define research and development, and the degree of detail you want to get into for the supporting business processes, it sounds like you've got somewhere between eight and twelve large business processes that your leaders would need to explicitly define in terms of inputs, outputs, key sub-steps, measures of performance and interdependencies. Is that doable?"

"Maybe," Lori answered. "I'll have to think about it more, but I'm beginning to see what you meant by level of detail."

"Fine," Peter said. "There'll be further opportunity to refer back to this template this afternoon, and even introduce others, as we explore BPM practices in more detail."

Harry, the logistics executive, broke in at that moment, "Before we move on, Peter, can I ask you something? We've found that some of our executives don't much care for process maps, and prefer tables and graphs. What's been your experience in this regard?"

"I've found that sometimes, too, Harry," Peter said. "In fact, I've developed a table format that captures basically the same information. Let me see if I have that slide here somewhere." He fiddled for a minute, "Ah, here it is."

Business Process	Input(s)	Key Steps	Output(s)	Functions Involved	Measures
Promotion	Growth strategies Budgets	Plan Implement Assess	Inquiries Orders	Marketing Sales Operations	Number of inquiries Cost per Inquiry
Product Order Fulfillment (Order to cash)	Orders	Record Pick, Pack Ship Invoice Collect	Cash	Sales Call Center Operations Procurement Finance	DSO % not perfect [1]
Service Order Fulfillment	Inquiries Orders	Record Quote Schedule Deliver	Cash	Sales Call Center Finance	DSO % not perfect [2]
Service Development	Growth strategies Budgets	Idea generation Feasibility Analysis Development Testing Launch	Orders	Consulting Marketing Finance Sales	Number of Orders % Revenue - New
Procurement	Forecasts Usage	Analyze Place orders Receive product Pay suppliers	Product	Procurement Operations Finance	Asset Utilization % product orders not perfect
Technology Deployment	Operational requirements Budgets	Monitor Assess Define Develop Implement Operate	Current and new functionality	IT All others	% downtime $ value created
Financial Reporting	Strategy Budgets Actuals	Gather data Analyze variances Prepare reports	Financial statements	Finance All others	Accuracy Timeliness

Enterprise Business Process View – ROSECO

Notes: 1. A perfect product order is defined as one which is complete, defect-free, delivered when requested and accompanied by an accurate invoice. 2. A perfect service order is defined as one which is provided when the customer asked for it, and works first time right.

"Thanks," Harry said, "that is useful. I like the chart format. For me, it provides a clearer link on which departments participate in which business processes to produce which results."

***

"So, we have just examined the importance of explicitly defining enterprise business processes. Leaders cannot implement business process management without deliberately and collaboratively developing this view of the business."

Now, let's direct our attention to the discussion of strategic focus," Peter continued. "In my view, one of the most challenging aspects of strategic focus is for an organization to develop a core strategy that *inspires* people throughout the company."

"When it comes to strategic focus, there is little debate as to what constitutes a core strategy. Most academics and business executives would agree on what this needs to include. But there are far too many 'cornflakes' strategies out there. Strategies that simply do not articulate in plain English how the company will win. Why do you think that is?"

"My experience is that we are often more concerned with the operating side of the business," Harry commented. "Strategy is something we feel we need to do once a year, present it to the board and then get back to our real jobs, which is running the business."

"We just don't dedicate enough quality time," Robin, the banking executive, said. "And we don't seem to have what it takes to make the tough choices on what to do, and what *not* to do. It sometimes seems as if we want to be all things to all people."

Glen was nodding agreement, "Amen to that! We tend to like models and buzzwords like 'product leadership' and 'operational excellence.' These terms may be meaningful to the leadership team, but they often don't sing to the people on the front lines."

"Those observations are right in line with my own experience," Peter remarked. "Buzzwords are a problem and people frequently complain about the lack of time."

"Maybe we're beginning to see that by explicitly defining customer requirements and *explicitly defining* enterprise business processes that will create value for customers, leaders can use the BPM framework to facilitate greater clarity on strategic direction and also provide the context to express it in terms that are more meaningful and concrete than platitudes and buzzwords."

"This afternoon we'll take a closer look at the second and third essential principles – the tight integration of strategy with the business process view and articulating strategy such that it inspires."

"That's it for this morning. I'd like to ask you to review and think about the workshop pre-reading items over lunch for this afternoon's discussion."

"Okay? Let's reconvene in an hour and a half, which should give you enough time to eat, read and reflect!"

Chapter 4: Building the Plan

As they left the room for lunch break, Bob turned to Glen and asked," Do you want to take a walk and clear our heads?"

"Good idea. Let's do that," Glen said.

As they walked through the lobby of the hotel, Bob quipped, "I think Peter really hit the nail on the head when he said that traditional thinking is a major problem."

"Yeah – but there's a good reason for that," Glen replied. "Just think. Back in our college days you were a computer science major and I was in engineering. Now, you're the CIO at your firm and I'm in charge of network operations at ours. That's true for most of our executive colleagues. Far too few of us have really meaningful cross-functional experience. We see the business from our turf."

"You're right," Bob added. "I see that in spades in terms of how our systems have evolved. I can't tell you how many siloed applications we're still saddled with, all that stuff we developed for the narrow needs of different departments. A lot of the time some of these managers are just thinking about how to run their own shop. They don't talk to one another at all, and I get stuck in the middle."

"I know, and it's amazing the way we perpetuate that. Just think of the way we talk about the other guy behind his back. You call the CFO a 'bean-counter,' she probably calls you a 'nerd.' Then there are 'schmoozers' and 'iron rings' – you know what I mean," Glen said.

"Yeah, and the consultants don't help much either. The marketing guys have their 'warfare' gurus. The finance guys have their 'scorecard' gurus. The purchasing guys have their 'supply chain' gurus. The manufacturing guys have their 'lean' gurus. Me, I get to listen to an endless line of sales pitches from the ERP gurus," Bob said.

"It's going to be tough to change all that, though," Glen reflected. "In a way it reminds me of the story of the city slicker who gets lost on country roads and stops to ask a farmer for directions. The farmer thinks for a minute, begins to speak a couple of times and stops in mid sentence each time. Then he finally says, 'Well, gosh darn it, I'm afraid that you just can't get there from here'."

"Let's hope it's not quite as bad as that," Bob said. "But it's certainly going to be difficult. We'll need some nourishment, just to talk about it. Let's grab a sandwich."

"Sounds good to me," Glen said. "Hey – did you see the big game last night?"

Over lunch, Bob and Glen proceeded to dissect the game, quarter by quarter.

    ***

Peter opened the afternoon session, "I thought we covered a lot of ground this morning. We talked in depth about what it means to look at the business from both the customer's view and the company's view, and we reviewed a couple of the key templates needed to launch enterprise business process management."

"While we touched on the second essential principle of assuring a tight integration of business process management with strategy, there's much more to discuss on this topic."

Peter powered up his laptop. "Assuming that the executive team has worked deliberately and collaboratively to explicitly define the enterprise framework, the key elements of this integration include the following:

- Using the data on customer requirements and current business process performance to prioritize strategic initiatives and assess the size of the gap to be bridged.
- Identifying which executives will be held accountable for business process performance improvement and process management.
- Developing a business process management plan that ties directly to the strategic direction of the firm."

"This paves the way to express strategic direction in business process terms."

Dave, the manufacturing executive, interrupted, "I can see how that might be helpful to an extent. But there are strategic issues where I just don't see the application of business process thinking. For example, we have some serious challenges around product pricing and segmentation. On top of that, in our custom manufacturing business, we are looking at acquiring one or two smaller firms to round out our presence on the west coast. I'm not clear on how business process management would help in these areas."

Peter replied, "As you say, there's a lot of complexity involved in strategy formulation. Certainly, there's much in management literature, including the pre-workshop reading assignments, which reinforce that. There are certain strategic decisions such as pricing, which products to offer to which market, and so on, where business process thinking may not play a central role. It is, however, the ability to execute on those decisions that counts, and that's where tightly integrating strategy to enterprise business processes comes in. On the other hand, the activities in making an acquisition or engaging in a merger can be represented in business process terms. I've seen organizations benefit from considering the M&A business process in terms of the cross-functional activities of planning, execution and integration."

Lori, the pharmaceutical company sales executive, spoke up. "I have a related question. You've now mentioned the need to appoint process owners a couple of times. I'm not sure our organization is culturally ready for that. Can't we launch business process management with our existing structure?"

Peter replied, "The assignment of business process owners doesn't mean you have to change your structure. Given the right circumstances, business process ownership can peacefully coexist with traditional functional roles. However, it is just as critical for the executive team to assign business process ownership roles as it is to assign functional roles. Otherwise, who would be accountable for monitoring and improving enterprise business process performance? Does that make sense?"

"To an extent, yes, I see what you mean," Lori said. But one could see by the expression on her face that she still had concerns.

Peter sensed that concern. "Maybe the balance of our conversation this afternoon and the case study will help clarify the point."

He continued, "The tight integration of business process management with strategy is simply a catalyst for gaining clarity on strategic direction. It's not a panacea for all that ails, but it can help leaders avoid what I've seen in some organizations, where developing strategy is like mating elephants – it takes place at a high level and involves a lot of bellowing."

"Maybe it makes sense to step back and think about the pre-workshop readings. What insights did you gain?"

"Well, of course, Porter talks about activities instead of business processes," Robin, the banking executive, noted. "But I can see why you asked us to read it. I got the sense there's a pretty strong parallel between BPM and Porter's treatment of activities, and that both can contribute to establishing competitive advantage."

Peter replied, "I think so, too. In fact, Porter first influenced my thinking when he introduced the concept of activities and the linkage to creating competitive advantage in his 1985 book, *Competitive Advantage*. But it was his 1996 HBR article, "What is Strategy?" that most concisely captured his thinking. I had observed, in my practical work, that competitive strategy is about being different by deliberately choosing a unique set of activities, and that this requires trade-offs and tough decisions, and perhaps most importantly, that it is the 'fit' between strategy, business process and organization design which most directly contributes to sustaining competitive advantage."

"I've always found it interesting that he avoids the use of the term business process. On the other hand, I've run into certain clients where 'process' has a bad name from failed reengineering efforts. With that in mind, I've used the term capability management as a proxy for business process management, simply to avoid the negative emotions around process."

Fred added, "I was really struck by the notion that while the various improvement initiatives such as TQM, reengineering, and other change management techniques may lead to operating improvements, companies have had difficulty in sustaining these gains. That's certainly been true for our railcar manufacturing firm. Just over the past eight years, I've seen initiatives such Kaizen, Lean Manufacturing and Activity Based Costing come and go. No wonder there'll be some skepticism if we move forward with BPM."

Peter smiled knowingly.

"Yeah, getting clarity on our priorities in our wireless business has been a big problem for us, too," Harry said. "In part I think this is due to the fact that our top team is basically a group of individuals with different functional backgrounds, and we tend to see priorities differently. So, I found the material from both Porter and Hamel on the need for trade-offs and the role of leadership pretty relevant. It made me realize that we must seize the opportunity to be more inventive and creative."

Peter elaborated, "I'm sure you've read about Southwest Airlines. The company was able to focus on the key sets of activities that facilitated the development of a profitable business in what is otherwise an industry where it's tough to make a profit. Maybe it's just luck that Dell was able to achieve unprecedented growth and profitability by changing the predominant business model in the PC industry from buy-make-sell-deliver-collect-service to sell-collect-buy-make-deliver-service. Somehow, I don't think so. I believe that Dell and Southwest and others have arrived at a defendable strategic position through the use of business process thinking."

"Since BPM prescribes that leaders arrive at the deliberate and collaborative definition, improvement and management of a firm's key business processes, it facilitates the development of a more distinct strategic position. It surfaces the areas of trade-offs where tough decisions need to be made, provides context to establish fit among the firm's sets of business processes and clarifies what needs to be improved and managed."

"BPM also provides a robust framework to make critical decisions around achieving competitive advantage – especially if we accept Porter's perspective that differentiation involves both the choice of activities and how they are carried out."

Peter said, "Now, before we get to the case study, let's take a few minutes to get your thoughts on the major pitfalls to avoid in achieving clarity on strategic direction. Please combine your own experience with the information in the reading assignments."

Fred, the marketing vice president, said, "Just from our experience, and with respect to looking at the business from the outside-in and inside-out, I'd like to suggest that one pitfall to avoid is failing to listen to the customer."

"I don't know if you've heard of us. Our company not only builds and leases railway cars, but we repair the cars as well," Fred continued. "We've known for several years that 80 percent of the root causes for a car being out of service or 'bad ordered' can be rectified right on the tracks. And, of course, our customers keep on asking us why we couldn't do that. We eventually did test and implement the use of mobile repair units, and now we not only have them nationwide but also they represent one of the fastest growing and most profitable parts of our business now. We've started to grow from our roots as a product company, to a 'product services' company offering total solutions for our customers."

"That's a good example," Peter said. "Most companies find it challenging to truly listen to customers, and more significantly, to take action. It brings up another important point, too."

"One of the principal areas for future growth is going to be providing product-related services. Maybe you've heard about the GE experience. Over the past decade, GE evolved from a primarily product-based company to a services company that also happens to make great products. Today, seventy percent of GE's revenues are estimated to come from product services."

"I've been thinking about that myself. Our big problem is that we've been too timid. Maybe we've even lost opportunities by not introducing some technical support services for our dealers. So, I'm starting to believe, as Hamel implied in his writing, that it's important to set aggressive goals – and setting modest growth goals is a pitfall to avoid," Fred said.

"It's interesting you should say that," Jim added. "I think our business may be guilty of that too. In the cable TV and high-speed Internet business, it's the Internet side of the business that's growing the fastest. Our technicians are pretty good at installing both services by now, but our customers have been asking, for some time now, why we can't offer related services, like setting up small home networks for homes with several computers. We keep on finding reasons, such as legal liability and workload scheduling, for not doing it. Yes, we're listening, but listening may not be enough, if all you do is make excuses why you can't do what the customer wants. If we had more aggressive goals, maybe it would change the way we look at these types of opportunities and drive us to action."

"That's very good," Peter commented while writing on the whiteboard. "You can listen to customers, but if you don't figure out a way to *execute* on what they tell you and in a timely manner, you're sunk."

"I'm wondering whether a related pitfall might be defining the scope of business too narrowly," Lori quizzed. "If an organization sets aggressive growth goals, the net has to be cast wide enough to capture related business opportunities. I think we are pretty good at that. We see ourselves as a producer and distributor of ethical pharmaceuticals – but that doesn't stop us from looking at related services."

"For example, one of our key drugs is the industry leader for controlled weight loss. A high percentage of patients who use this drug also have other health issues, such as diabetes, heart disease and sleep apnea. So when we noticed a couple of fledgling organizations that provide counseling services by both phone and e-mail to patients with severe weight loss challenges, we saw a chance to cross-market and expand. We have talked a lot about 'disease management' – which is basically our jargon for having a holistic view on how to serve an entire therapeutic area, and we are now starting to define the scope of our services broadly enough to include taking a position with this type of service."

"That reminds me of something else I wanted to say," Lori continued. "In the pharmaceutical business, it seems we are masters of 'buzzwords and jargon.' That's something we talked about earlier, the excessive use of buzzwords and jargon. Two years ago, for example, we had a strategy document that stated we would excel at five key capabilities: 'customer interface,' 'relationship management,' 'program development,' and 'disease management,' which I was just talking about. . . . Gosh, I've forgotten the fifth one. Well, that tells you something, doesn't it?"

"The problem was that the members of the leadership team were the only ones who understood what those terms meant in terms of what needed to be done and who would do it. I doubt whether this document was meaningful to the front line and it sure didn't provide the kind of guidance I needed with respect to daily decision-making. This year's strategy document is much better, though, I have to say."

A number of people nodded at these comments.

"I know what you mean," Fred added. "It's awfully easy to fall into using buzzwords. Several of the top people at my company were influenced a lot by Treacy and Wiersema's book, *The Discipline of Market Leaders*, that talks about strategic position in terms of choosing between what they call 'value disciplines,' 'customer intimacy,' 'product leadership,' or 'operational excellence.' You have to pick which one to excel at and then work to maintain your performance in the other two."

"This template seemed to suit our business, and I think that it still does, but we really went overboard with the slogans. We had them pasted everywhere. Then we had a tough year, and our people started getting the feeling that the 'operational excellence' we were talking about was just an innocent-sounding way of saying layoffs and cutbacks – kind of like the euphemism of 'downsizing' used to let go of people during the business reengineering decade. It's tough to avoid the use of a certain amount of jargon, but we should make sure that it's clear to all and that we don't go overboard."

"What Fred just said has helped me think of another pitfall," Harry said. "In our agricultural equipment company, I think we try to do too much. We end up having this thick strategy document with virtually dozens of so-called strategic initiatives. We don't have sufficient clarity around what is truly strategic. We start a broad range of initiatives, and then a number of them just fall off the table due to lack of resources or sponsorship. The pitfall to avoid is 'Not making the tough choices' with respect to the few critical strategic initiatives."

Peter commented, "That's actually fairly common, Harry."

Bob joined in, "We've had the same problem in the past. Recently, in our chemical business we've found that limiting the number of strategic initiatives also helps to keep the key priorities in front of our people throughout the year and installing rewards that really have impact. It also helps avoid another pitfall – not linking the strategic initiatives to operating plans and budgeting."

Peter finished scribbling on the whiteboard. "Well, that gives us several pitfalls to avoid. Why don't we review these and see if they still make sense:

- Failing to listen to customers.
- Setting goals that are too modest to drive innovation.
- Defining the scope of business too narrowly.
- Excessive use of jargon or buzzwords.
- Trying to do too much – not making the tough choices.

▪ Not making a commitment to link strategic initiatives to operating plans, budgets, and management rewards."

"Now, while we have been talking about pitfalls, I'm sure you'd agree that flipping these around from negative to positive provides us with a list of opportunities. So, let's look at how leaders can employ the BPM framework to avoid some of these pitfalls or help capitalize on opportunities, and how it can provide guidance on tactical decisions and a context for establishing fit or alignment."

"But, let's be clear on a few key points. First, the BPM framework of deliberately and collaboratively defining the corporation's business processes should ideally precede or be done concurrently with the development of strategy – not as an afterthought. This is a leadership decision. "

"There are also some things that BPM won't do, such as enhancing the degree of innovation, calibrating the aggressiveness of your goals, increasing the degree of discipline in gathering environmental data and improving the way you price your products and services. But, there's a lot of guidance out there to help with these challenges. In addition to Hamel's 1996 HBR article, 'Strategy as Revolution,' which you've read, I'll direct you toward some additional reading on these topics on your resources list at the end of the session today."

"What BPM *does* provide is this. Given a set of data, it provides a robust way of evaluating the decisions you have to make about your key strategic initiatives."

"Further, the BPM framework creates the context in which leaders can express strategy in concrete business process terms. It facilitates answering some extremely relevant questions:

- Which business processes need to be improved – and by how much – in order to achieve our strategic objectives?
- What are the key measures of performance we will need to monitor?
- Which executives will be accountable for the performance of critical business processes?
- How will they be rewarded?"

"After the break, we'll look at the case of a regional mortgage company, REMOCO, in order to illustrate the thought process involved. I'd suggest we take a half-hour break. That should be enough time to look at the case study materials."

***

After the group had reconvened, Peter continued. "The case assignment is essentially designed to develop the answers to four questions.

- Which business processes need to be improved – and by how much – in order to achieve our strategic objectives?
- What are the key measures of performance we will need to monitor?
- Which executives will be accountable for the performance of critical business processes?
- What are the key initiatives in the business process management plan?"

"Just a word of caution, the case, like the real world, does have some missing information. So we'll have to make some assumptions as we proceed."

"Given that we have less than an hour and a half left today, I propose that we work together to prepare a response to each of the assigned questions. Okay?"

Everyone nodded their agreement.

"Okay," Peter said," the first question about REMOCO is which business processes need to be improved, and by how much, in order to achieve the company's strategic objectives? Who wants to kick it off?"

"I'll take a stab at it," Fred, the marketing executive, said. "I thought the case materials implied pretty clearly which business processes need to be improved, but they were less clear on the point of 'by how much.' REMOCO's vision is 'peerless service,' right? It operates as an independent division of a regional bank, as an independent business unit. It has fairly aggressive targets in terms of increases in unit volume, customer satisfaction and profitability. Its core, customer-touching, business processes have been defined by their executive team as Promotion, Sales, Mortgage Processing and Mortgage Administration."

"Each of these business processes clearly requires improvement, based on what's in the case materials. Making some assumptions, I believe that the company would need to reduce the average cost of processing and administering a mortgage by 15 to 20 percent or more. I can also see that the sales process needs improvement, but I'm not quite sure by how much."

"Thanks, Fred," Peter said. "Anyone want to add to what Fred has said?"

Jim, the CFO, said, "I was thinking about what we discussed this morning. Maybe looking at the measurement question can shed some more light on this."

"Fine," Peter replied. "What are your thoughts on that, Jim?"

Jim replied, "While REMOCO clearly has to reduce the cost of mortgage processing and administration, that's not going to get them to their financial targets. I think there's some data missing here. Still, it's clear that the output of the promotions process is inquiries and that the key metric is volume of inquiries. The sales process converts those inquiries into qualified mortgage applications, and the company's main metrics are cycle time, from application to approval, and cost per application. So, they are going to have to either get the same number of inquiries or leads at a lower cost, or increase the number of leads with the same promotions dollar investment, or find a way to convert more leads into applications at a lower cost."

"I made a few quick calculations and my sense is that, given the case material on market conditions, they're best off in targeting more inquiries at the same investment level. Now, going on to the other measures, the Mortgage Processing business process – that's a mouthful – converts applications into closed and funded loans. Cycle time is less meaningful here because some properties close quickly, while others, such as new homes under construction, don't. On the other hand, both cost per application and customer satisfaction are critical measures. Finally, with respect to the Mortgage Administration process, the key measures seem to be the average cost to administer, accuracy of monthly transactions, and customer satisfaction."

"I think there are a couple of other quality-related measures which would be useful for this regional mortgage company to monitor. First of all, the completeness and accuracy of applicant information at the end of the sales process would be an important thing to measure, as that will impact the amount of redundant effort in the mortgage processing process. Also, the completeness and accuracy of the final documents at closing would also be a key metric for the mortgage processing process as it may impact the average cost of administering the mortgage. Sorry I've rambled a bit, but that's what happens when you get a finance guy on a case like this."

As Peter finished writing Jim's input on the whiteboard, he said, "Those are solid additions Jim. Thanks. Does anyone have more to add on this measurement point?"

Lori spoke up, "I'm not sure, but it seems to me that the measures of customer satisfaction should capture the entire customer experience as well as the specific level of customer satisfaction with respect to key business processes."

"I'd agree with that," Peter replied. "Further, it's interesting to note that the case does not have much information on the supporting business processes. Even though the parent organization supplies some of the key enabling services in terms of information technology and human resources, there should be a set of end-of-process measures for these business processes."

"I'm glad you mentioned that," Bob, the chemical company CIO, said. "I wanted to explore the role of information technology in all this. The case book says that IT services are provided by the parent company's resources. In this instance, who would own the IT development process? What performance measures would apply?"

Peter answered, "In the REMOCO scenario, the IT development process, and for that matter, other enabling business processes, such as recruiting, financial reporting and purchasing, would be owned and managed by executives in the parent company. Still, REMOCO would want to make sure that they are getting good value for the cross-charges that apply with respect to these services. The BPM model really places this in perspective. It creates context for the development of performance criteria on both the operation of information systems and the development of new functionality. Given the BPM model, REMOCO could negotiate service level agreements on operating factors such as 'system availability,' and 'help desk responsiveness.' It could influence the company to develop applications like automated underwriting, storage of imaged property appraisal documents and so on. BPM practices guide executive thinking in the direction of how enabling technology can actually improve business process performance."

Bob added, "I'd argue that REMOCO would not be able to achieve its cost reduction goals in mortgage processing without deploying technology solutions such as automated underwriting and imaging. So we should add those to the business process plan. On the other hand, there's no information in the case to indicate issues around HR or financial reporting."

"Yes, that's probably right. It also leads us to another insight. The leaders of a business unit would be ill-advised to embark on the BPM road without the clear-cut support of shared service organizations housed in corporate," Peter said, as he addressed Bob's comment. "Now, what about the process ownership question?"

Harry, the logistics executive, spoke up, "Okay, here's how I see it. REMECO is organized around traditional functional lines. In addition to the CEO, there's a VP Sales, VP Call Center, VP Operations, VP Credit and VP Administration. So, the ownership issue is clear for three of the four core business processes. What's not clear is who should own the promotion process and what the role of the VP Call Center and the VP Credit should be. I'd suggest that the VP Sales should be accountable for both the Promotions and the Sales process, since the Director of Marketing reports to the VP Sales, and maybe the VP Call Center should be a co-owner of the Sales process."

"That might work, Peter said, "although my experience has been that the workload involved in owning more than one enterprise process is very difficult to manage. Also, the joint ownership of business processes presents its own set of challenges. The key point to remember is that *we are talking about owning the end-to-end business processes*, as Lori and I discussed this morning, and not reporting relationships and functional performance. So, the focus is on the flow of cross-functional activities. To illustrate, consider how the performance of the mortgage processing business process relies upon activities from both the sales and call center organizations in terms of clarifying applicant information, as well as upon third parties, for property appraisals, and the credit department for guidelines on risk assessment."

"Now, let's see if we can get closure on some of the details so we can complete the business process management plan that I've started to flesh out on the whiteboard."

The discussion of the regional mortgage company, RE-MOCO, case continued until they had agreed on the answers to the key questions, and Peter drew the following table on the whiteboard.

Business Process	*	Output	Measures	Performance Gap	Process Owner	Likely Action
Promotion	C	Inquiries	Number of inquiries Cost per inquiry	Cost per inquiry is too high	Director of Marketing	Improve
Sales	C	Completed Mortgage Applications	% conversion Revenue Accuracy Completeness Timeliness	% conversion from inquiry to completed application too low Too many completed applications are missing data or not accurate	VP Sales	Improve
Mortgage Processing	C	Closing and funded loans	On time Complete & accurate Cost per unit Customer Satisfaction	Cost per unit too high, maybe by as much as 20%	VP Operations	Redesign
Mortgage Administration	C		Per unit cost # errors		VP Administration	Manage
Technology Development	E	Existing and new functionality	Downtime Help desk responsiveness Value added	Need new applications to reduce cost per unit of mortgage processing	CIO	Improve
Financial Reporting	E	Not yet addressed				
Recruiting	E	Not yet addressed				

Draft BPM Plan – REMOCO Case Exercise
* Note: C - denotes a core process, E - denotes an enabling process

Then, Peter summarized, "Thank you for some excellent work. Hopefully, this case has helped reinforce what it means to tightly integrate BPM with strategy."

"While our group solution for the REMOCO business management plan isn't perfect, it does illustrate the key concepts in tightly linking business process management with strategy. This is what makes the application of BPM exciting; as the leadership team discusses which business processes need to be improved by how much to achieve strategic objectives and who will be accountable for getting it done. Does anyone have any final questions or comments on this case?"

"I just have a comment," Lori said. "I think I'm getting closer to understanding the concept of business process ownership. It isn't really about reporting responsibility, is it? It's got much more to do with influencing other functional areas to work on the performance of the enterprise business process and getting results through collaboration and measurement. Is that right?"

Peter smiled. "Excellent, you've cut to the chase, Lori." "You're right on track. But there's more, and we'll get to those further details on Process Ownership tomorrow."

***

"Now, I'd suggest we examine the third essential principle in implementing BPM which is to articulate the firm's strategy such that it *inspires,* from the boardroom to the lunchroom, and remains front and center throughout the year."

"Just consider how the leadership at REMOCO could weave critical and meaningful information into the company's strategy communications, and modify its measurement and reward systems accordingly. They could make specific reference to the company objectives around improving the yield of promotional programs, capturing applicant information first-time-right, reducing the cost of processing applications by introducing appropriate technology, and better partnering with third party providers of related service. Imagine how that might work. Consider how it would help individuals to clarify their roles in closing the performance gap in a given enterprise business process. Then, ask yourselves to what extent is that done within your own organizations?"

Peter paused for a moment.

Fred, the marketing executive, said," I'm not sure that *saying* that 'we are committed to BPM' is any better than saying 'we're committed to operational excellence' as a key strategic initiative."

Peter replied," No, it's not. I'd discourage leaders from positioning it in that way. Companies who elect to position BPM as just another initiative are likely to find that they won't get much more than they did from their prior TQM, reengineering or activity based costing initiatives. I'm referring to zeroing in and articulating the plans to close gaps in performance from both a customer's and a company's point of view. I maintain that this thought model and the linkage to key business processes enable an organization to articulate strategic direction in a way that is more meaningful to employees."

Jim said, "Okay. I can see that. But doesn't balanced scorecard do that, too?"

"To a certain extent, it does," Peter answered. "However, in my view the balanced scorecard doesn't make a sufficiently explicit linkage between business process performance and customer requirements. But if you are already using a version of the balanced scorecard, you can create that explicit connection by simply asking which business processes need to be improved, and by how much, in order to achieve our goals in the customer quadrant, financial quadrant and so on. So there is room for the two approaches to work hand in glove. In fact, some emerging BPM information systems already claim to have the means to 'build-in' the balanced scorecard measures."

"Wouldn't confidentiality be an issue?" Harry asked. "I mean does it make sense to release potentially sensitive information to employees?"

Bob interjected, "I believe it does. But that's for each organization to decide. An option might be to articulate these goals in terms of percentage of improvement. I've seen that work."

"I'd agree with that," Peter added. "There's a lot to be said for what I believe General Patton once said, 'Never tell people how to do things. Tell them what to do and they will surprise you with their ingenuity.' That fits right in with BPM principles."

"If there are no more questions or comments for the moment, I'd like to summarize this section and speak to the reading assignment for this evening."

***

"During today's discussion on strategic focus, we have considered the first three essential principles of business process management."

---

1) Look at the business from the *outside-in,* from the customer's perspective, as well as from the *inside-out.*
2) Tightly integrate strategy with enterprise business processes.
3) Articulate strategy to inspire, from the boardroom to the lunchroom.

We have explored how leaders can employ the BPM framework to create context for strategic decision-making.

By explicitly defining the core business processes, including inputs, key steps, outputs and key measures of performance, the likelihood of looking at the business from both the company's and the customer's point of view is increased. When this is supplemented by an assessment of the current performance of core business processes, it equips the executive team to express the organization's strategy in business process terms, by specifying the size of the gap that needs to be closed in order to achieve strategic objectives. This framework can be used to gain more clarity on the choice of activities and how they will be performed. It fits well with some of the key concepts outlined by Porter and will appeal to those who believe that the essence of strategy involves decisions or choices on performing activities differently than the competition."

"The BPM framework also assists leaders in avoiding some of the pitfalls we identified. By expressing strategy in terms of business processes and the performance gaps that need to be bridged, leaders can minimize the use of jargon and buzzwords. Strategic direction then has a better chance of being understood by everyone, and the groundwork can be established to keep strategic issues front and center throughout the year. The business process management plan is the key vehicle that can be used for this purpose."

"The BPM framework furthermore sets the stage for leaders to make tough choices and creates a context in which strategic initiatives can be tightly linked to operating plans, budgets and management rewards, as we will see in the next two days."

"But BPM is neither substitute for innovative thinking and creativity along the lines that Hamel emphasizes, nor a robust strategy development methodology to address the full range of strategic decisions."

***

"In tomorrow's session, we'll look at how an organization can best align its resources to deliver on strategic objectives based on business process thinking. Alignment or 'fit' is what 'locks out imitators' as Porter points out. We'll see that clarity on strategic direction in business process terms is an absolute prerequisite in this regard, and that the four cornerstones of alignment are 1) business process design, 2) organization structure, 3) process measurement, and 4) incentives."

"We'll also talk about the three essential principles related to organizational alignment. These require that a company take action to:

4) Design enterprise business processes to deliver on strategic goals.
5) Ensure that the organization design enables enterprise business process execution.
6) Deploy enabling technology based on the value added through enhanced business process performance."

"This evening's reading assignments are on the table at the back of the room. They include a couple of articles by Michael Hammer that address the topic of Process Ownership and the increasing need to look at cross-company business processes, and an interesting article by Ross and Weill on some decisions IT people shouldn't make. We will be referring to some of their key concepts during tomorrow's session. You will also find a resource list including additional recommended reading for the future. For future reference, those of you who are interested in a concise overview of the strategy process may wish to look at Chapter Four in Alan Brache's book, *How Organizations Work*. You'll also note a number of interesting and complementary articles cited on the resource list."

"Thanks for a good day, and I'll see you in the morning."

Reading Assignments

Hammer, Michael, "The Superefficient Company," *Harvard Business Review*, September 2001.

Hammer, Michael and Steven Stanton, "How Process Enterprises Really Work," *Harvard Business Review*, November – December 1999, pgs 108-118.

Ross, Jeanne W. and Peter Weill, "Six IT Decisions Your IT People Shouldn't Make," *Harvard Business Review*, November 2002, pgs 84-91.

***

"After picking up the handouts and exchanging a few words with Glen and a couple of the other participants, Bob approached Peter and asked, "Peter, do you have a few minutes?"

"Sure, I've got time for a quick question or two," Peter replied.

"I just wanted to hear a bit more on your views about the viability of the business process languages outlined in the Smith and Fingar book. I didn't want to get into the technical aspects during the session," Bob said.

Peter said, "Fine, shoot."

"Okay," Bob said. "Well, let me just outline the little I know from skimming their book and then ask a question. My understanding is that the new business process languages are specifications both for building process management systems and for modeling business processes. Such business process languages can provide the required abstract model for all processes, along with a standards-based XML schema and syntax for expressing and managing business processes. So, I guess my first question is this. In your view, where are such languages in practical terms?"

Peter replied, "Just to build on what you've said, I draw analogies that business process languages are to shared business processes what XML is for shared business data and HTML is for hyperlinked Web pages. Now we have business process modeling companies retooling to sit on top of business process languages. The robustness of these tools will have a direct impact on the extent to which process models will be *directly executable* by BPM systems. From a business perspective, that means that once a business process has been designed, it can be deployed immediately – as you well know, Bob, that's exciting. It's potentially a radical breakthrough."

Bob asked, "Since such systems aren't widely known and deployed right now, is the jury still out, or at least for the time being?"

"My guess is that the growth and maturity of BPM systems and technologies will follow a similar pattern to the way database management systems were developed and assimilated two decades ago. On the other hand, early adopters are already claiming attention-grabbing ROI numbers from BPM technologies, right in the midst of the current economic downturn. It seems to me it's time to put a stake in the ground, pilot these systems, and grow their deployment in step with the forthcoming technology developments over the coming decade. It's certainly not a bet-the-farm proposition. Yet one should be aware that, *not* to make the move could mean costly catch up and competitive disadvantage. So, maybe the jury is still out, but companies that 'get it' are not waiting for a courtroom verdict. Companies like GE with its Digitization Initiative, are believed to have already documented the business case – and acted. GE is determined to optimize all of its business processes, using every available BPM tool, to dominate its industries. I certainly wouldn't want to have to play catch up against GE if I were competing in one of its industries," Peter replied.

"Okay. As you can imagine, in the real world, which I see daily, actual application development involves translating business process designs into an IT deliverable, through a complex and unwieldy procedure. I get requirements 'thrown over the wall' for us to somehow figure out how to implement, often with distorted results. So, how do you think the BPM technology will differ from the traditional IT model?" Bob asked.

Peter thought for a moment, "You probably know better than I that the IT industry has been trying for two decades to streamline the translation of business requirements into business objects and then into code. Now there's new hope if Smith and Fingar's book is on the mark. Imagine that a rich process-representation language can express any process, and a dedicated execution environment can immediately put new processes to work. Third-wave process management is a straight-through process – no physical translation into executable code is required. As a result, process systems can be tuned live. Simulation and analysis are expected to be able to be performed on-line in the context of live business operations. Process improvement initiatives can be measured and analyzed, which makes evaluating the return on process investment (ROPI) far more scientific. Business therefore gets the process model it wants, a model that need not be translated or distorted in any way."

"That's my understanding as well," Bob said. "This is exactly why your approach on executive thinking around BPM is so timely. But, 'Once bitten, twice shy.' What concerns me is the flexibility of the BPM technology. For example, when the business process changes, how does BPM technology adapt?"

"That's a common concern, and a good one," Peter said. "Again, all this stuff is pretty new, but in theory the BPM technology contemplates that all participants can share process designs, and changes can be propagated across systems and business partners. Actually, I see this as a must-have. One of the most challenging and costly problems faced by companies today is change management, closely related to process lifecycle management, since each change request can be viewed as a process instance in its own right."

"You can say that again," Bob confirmed.

Peter continued, "BPM technology hopes to provide the capability to manage the entire lifecycle of the change management process from design to deployment to execution to continuous improvement. The change-management process design should incorporate all the participants in the change, including employees, value-chain partners, systems and other processes. It should also be able to model both the automated and manual interactions in a single environment. Does that answer your question?"

"Yes it does," Bob said, "and I definitely have some homework to do on this topic after the workshop."

"All right," Peter replied. "While we probably don't want to get into this level of technical detail during the workshop, it's probably a good idea to raise the group's level of awareness of this evolving technology, especially during tomorrow's session on alignment."

"I agree," Bob said. "Well, have a good evening."

"You too. I'll see you in the morning."

Chapter 5: Creating Fit

The next morning, as Fred got out of his car at the hotel parking lot, he noticed that Harry was parking just a couple of spots away. Fred waited a minute for Harry and they began the short walk to the hotel's conference center.

Harry asked, "Fred, what did you think of the assigned reading?"

"Actually, I just scanned it briefly. I spent most of the evening thinking about this bit on how to express strategy such that it *inspires* people throughout the company. I think White's got something of value there. In our railcar business, we need to get more specific in our communication and I'm beginning to see how we might do that," Fred said.

"What do you mean?" Harry asked.

"While I'm not sure we know all the issues, we sure are clear about some of the big ones," Fred replied. "Things like increasing the percent of orders received over the Web, getting orders right the first time, reducing the cost of engineering through the use of our intranet-based design tool and so on. I'm starting to see that by measuring and managing our performance in business process terms we can rally our folks around, we can really make some progress on these issues."

"Interesting," Harry said. "I'm with you in principle. That would be better than the jargon-packed platitudes we've sometimes used in our parts distribution business. But I'm still from Missouri, you know, the 'show me state.' Maybe it's got something to do with my need for detail and my engineering background."

They walked through the lobby and into the meeting room, which was already buzzing with casual conversation, and went over to the breakfast buffet.

Once everyone had settled into their seats, Peter began. "Let's start where we left off. Business process thinking can make a significant contribution to strategic focus, as I hope everyone came to see in the case study, as well as the discussion around the first three essential principles of business process management. The effective application of these three principles results in:

- Better clarity on what customers require.
- A business process management plan indicating the degree of improvement required for the core business processes to achieve strategic targets, and the assignment of business process ownership.
- Key themes and messages to communicate major initiatives in business process terms."

"Now, today's agenda will take us to the topic of organizational alignment. We will have a series of discussions and two exercises to explore the next three essential principles intrinsic to enterprise management. Stated slightly differently, these are:

- Assure that the organization's core enterprise business processes are designed to deliver on its strategic goals.
- Ensure that the organization design, as defined by the structure, measures, and rewards, enables effective business process execution.
- Assess and deploy enabling technology based on the value added through enhanced business process performance."

Peter continued, "Arriving at organizational alignment requires a further level of detail around the definition and performance of the critical business processes that create value. It requires that action be taken such that the organization's core business processes are designed to deliver on the strategic priorities."

"That reminds me. A question occurred to me last night with respect to strategic focus. How many business processes need to be analyzed and what level of detail is needed for the leadership team to achieve this close integration of strategy with business process performance?" Harry asked.

"That's a terrific question, and a tough one, too," Peter said.

"The stock-in-trade answer is that 'it depends.' My view is that initially the enterprise-level work requires only that an organization identify its *core* enterprise business processes, and direct the analysis on those. The number of business processes will vary somewhat from one business to the next, but it's generally accepted that most companies have only five-to-eight *core* business processes."

"Take manufacturing companies. They typically develop it, buy it, make it, sell it, deliver it, and service it. More formally stated they will usually have product development, procurement, manufacturing, sales, order fulfillment, information technology development, performance management, and maybe one or two others specific to the business they're in. Service companies will have a similar set, with service delivery instead of manufacturing. The same goes for technology providers, which might also add network development and operation to the list of core processes. Now, with respect to the level of detail, I'd suggest that a high-level analysis would suffice."

"That still sounds like an awful lot of work to me," Harry said. "We just can't put our business on hold while we're doing this. Do you know what I mean?"

"Indeed, I do," Peter replied, "and I'd suggest that the scope of this level of analysis doesn't require you to put your business on hold. We'll be doing a case study later this morning that should provide you with some insight on the next level down, the mid-level level of analysis. However, since this is clearly an area of concern, let's spend a few minutes on it right now."

"Let's explore what this might involve on a practical basis. I've observed that most senior managers can readily articulate their understanding of business goals, their understanding of the major business processes and the key issues. Would anyone care to provide us with an example of this based on his or her organization – without revealing any state secrets of course?"

Jim spoke up, "I'll take a shot at it. Our cable TV and high speed ISP business' goals are as follows:
- Achieve certain levels of revenues, operating margin and EBITDA.
- Ensure that we carry out installations on time and first time right.
- Ensure reliable service.
- Provide exemplary customer service.
- Build market share in the 'small business – commercial' segment to achieve target levels."

"So, I see the key business processes for our firm to be the promotion process, the sales process, the order fulfillment process (including the installation process), the customer service process, and the network operations and management process."

"Okay, Jim. If these business processes continued to perform at current levels, is the firm likely to achieve its goals?" Peter asked.

"Well, that's a good question," Jim replied. "We seem to be having a problem in hitting our 'on-time, first-time-right' objectives for the installation of our high speed Internet product and our new subscriber growth rates among small businesses is behind plan – but I believe we can make up the lost ground in the next few months."

"What seem to be the issues around *on-time, first-time-right*, Peter asked?

"We're not absolutely sure, but the current thinking is that it involves several factors. First, we believe that our order taking practices need to be improved to assure that we don't accept orders from people who have computer equipment that doesn't meet the minimum systems requirement for broadband Internet access. Then, we seem to have an issue around meeting scheduled installation windows, and there are concerns about the training our technicians get on modem installation."

"As I'm speaking, it occurs to me that we should take a harder look at the cross-functional activities, roles and responsibilities, and measures needed to take 'perfect orders,' so to speak, and execute 'perfect installations.' We need to get a better handle on the root causes of defects in execution and better understand the variances in performance."

"Thanks, Jim," Peter said. "We just saw that, when prompted, Jim easily and naturally described the performance of business processes around the critical issues in order fulfillment including reference to the next level of detail in some of the sub-processes. Harry, would you be willing to participate in this experiment?"

Harry was deep in thought. After a moment he perked up, "Okay, our division provides heavy equipment spare parts to dealers of agricultural and construction equipment. Generally, the division's strategic goals are:
- Achieve target revenues and operating margin.
- Deliver orders on-time, complete, and defect free.
- Grow the technical service support side of our business to pre-set targets.
- Provide exceptional customer service."

"So, our key business processes include order fulfillment, supply chain management and customer service. In the customer service process, we're looking mainly at providing first-time-right information and the key activities are inquiry handling, investigation and response. We are doing pretty well in terms of responding to technical questions and general inquiries. To anticipate your question, Peter, one of the major issues we're painfully aware of relates to backorders. Due to the long shelf life of our equipment and various model changes, we need to manage the inventory for a very broad range of parts and accessories. When stock of a component is depleted, we need to get our manufacturing division to build it. However, their priorities are not always the same as ours."

Harry paused for a moment, then said, "I'm beginning to see what you mean."

"Thanks, Harry," Peter went on. "So the issue is not that the high-level business process analysis takes a ton of effort. Instead, the challenge is for the executive team to see things the same way and take action on what's truly important. That's partly why I say that business process management is a *team sport*. As Harry said, the manufacturing organization's priorities are not the same as the part's division's priorities."

"The key point is this. *Strategy should drive business process design and business process design should drive organization design.* However, far too often, a traditional thought model dominates executive thinking, where turf trumps performance. This becomes an even greater challenge as a company takes steps to work on alignment issues, where a more detailed-level of business process analysis is needed."

"In fact, even those organizations that have learned to focus in, systematically, on one or two key business processes do not necessarily know how to think about their business systemically in business process terms."

"But don't just take my word for it. Let's do a quick thought experiment together. Robin, let's start with you. Has your organization successfully redesigned any major business process?"

Robin responded, "Actually, yes. We reengineered our corporate lending process and got some really good improvement in compressing the cycle time for approving loans. We got a nice level of cost reduction, too."

It was Jim's turn next. "We did some reengineering a few years ago, if that's what you mean, but that was before my time."

"My turn?" Harry asked. "We redesigned the dealer inquiry process a few years ago. Data accuracy and responsiveness wound up looking a lot better. But, as I said, we never did solve the parts backorder problem, and so in some cases, we simply ended up developing the means to give dealers bad news faster."

"Our company has done a lot of process improvement on the supply chain process and I am pleased to say we achieved some solid cost savings. In fact, we're regarded as one of the leaders in the chemical industry when it comes to supply chain management," Bob explained.

"We redesigned the way we did network management, but I have to say, the results were pretty mediocre for all the work and time my people put into it," Glen added.

Fred commented, "Our sales process for new railcar sales needed attention, so we tackled that. We got pretty good results in terms of the time it takes to turn quotations around, but if you ask me, there's room for a lot more improvement."

Lori continued, "That sounds a bit like what we did with our order to cash process in getting drugs to pharmacists, but I think we actually did focus in on some of the right things, order accuracy, the volume of back orders, and the bottlenecks that impacted the cost of doing that piece of the operation."

Dave added, "We haven't done much in the way of process improvement work."

"Okay," Peter remarked. "Well, that gives us a pretty good idea. It seems that in several cases there has been some positive experience with process improvement on at least one major business process."

"Now, let's reflect on the role of leadership in implementing enterprise thinking. My claim, as you know, is that success in one or two process improvement efforts does not mean that the executive team has 'got it' when it comes to enterprise-wide process thinking. Bob and Fred – you seem to be enthusiastic about how process improvement worked for your companies."

"So let me ask you, did the leadership team go on to develop a shared understanding of the key business processes that delivered value to customers? Were they linked to strategic goals using jargon-free language? Were the inputs, the key sub-steps, and the outputs of these business processes well defined? Was there an enterprise process management plan developed? Was the performance of the full set of core processes measured and reported monthly? Were the major processes explicitly defined, and did they take into account the linkages with other critical processes? Did you implement standing cross-group teams, led by executives with broad accountability and meaningful rewards, dedicated to managing and improving those business processes?"

"Whoa! That's a pretty tall order," Bob, exclaimed, smiling wryly. "But I get your point. We've done some good things on supply chain, but we're not even close to doing all of these things on an enterprise level."

Fred added, "That goes for us too."

"Okay. If you'll excuse the Yogism, for me this is déjà vu – all over again. Even when there's been positive experience with process improvement, management teams often don't replicate the outcome on a company-wide basis. They don't take what would seem to be 'the logical next step.' This also gives us some insight about Lori's stated interest in implementing BPM from the bottom up. It's not impossible, but the odds are against it unless senior management is committed to managing the enterprise business processes and the BPM tools and methods are universally available –

one of the most radical of third-wave BPM concepts. Top-level business processes represent the tip of the iceberg, and the full range of supporting processes must also be brought under the umbrella of BPM, for BPM must be applied systemically throughout the enterprise."

"One additional indicator of the receptiveness to business process thinking in the management environment is to explore where the members of the executive team spend most of their time and effort."

"Glen, remind us what you said customers in the wireless industry are demanding. Let me check my notes. You said 'variety, value for money, hassle-free activation, reliable service, ease of payment, and ready access to knowledgeable customer support.' Is that about right?"

"That's it," Glen nodded.

"Okay, so where would you say your management team spends more time? Is it in discussing topics such as subscriber additions, churn rates, technology [e.g. GSM, TDMA, new phone designs, pricing plan issues and so on], and budget to actual performance? Or is it spent discussing the key steps and opportunities in retail channel partner management, the performance of the activation process, the degree of service reliability as evidenced by items such as the coverage you are offering, the potential for application of enabling technology in core business processes and the responsiveness rating of your customer support services?"

"I'd have to say we spend the majority of our time on the former area," Glen kind of mumbled.

"In my experience that's true for most organizations. Where the leadership spends most of its time says a lot about what it thinks is really important," Peter emphasized.

"That's why it's essential to create a management environment where it is common and natural to ask key questions around performance in business process terms."

"Let me backtrack for a moment. As we saw a few minutes ago, even organizations with a successful experience in business process improvement, do not necessarily have the ability to think about business processes systemically. Why is this?"

"I'd suggest to you that the primary reasons are the following. First, the functional mindset still rules in most organizations, and turf protection is widespread. Second, many executives still don't understand business processes at the enterprise level. To them, business processes are simply a set of mechanical steps and procedures that the 'quality people' do. Third, and perhaps most importantly, most organizations still have reward systems that are based on functional excellence and not linked to business process performance."

"Finding the right balance between functional and process thinking is certainly one of the most significant management challenges of our time, and as we'll discuss later today, that challenge is likely to be compounded by the need to extend business process management practices across company boundaries for critical, end-to-end, business processes."

***

"That said, I'd like to return to the role business process thinking should play in organizational alignment."

"First, let's recall that I define 'organizational alignment' as the degree of 'fit' between an organization's strategic direction, its business processes, its structure, performance measures and rewards."

"Exploring issues around the degree of fit requires more detailed analysis of the firm's business processes. Typically, this is best done by business process management teams, working under the direction of each Process Owner, and involves asking and answering a set of questions, including the following:

- What major performance gaps or 'business issues' exist?
- Does the current organization structure enable effective business process execution – avoiding unnecessary hand-offs, for example?
- Is our measurement system sufficiently comprehensive to serve the needs of the business?
- Are we rewarding behavior that's most likely to produce the desired outcomes?
- What enabling technology is likely to be required to improve business process performance?"

"Teams will find this 'performance-gap' or 'business-issue' driven approach useful in working toward organizational alignment."

"I'm curious, had I simply asked you what comes immediately to mind when the term organizational alignment is mentioned, what would you have said?"

Bob replied, "I would have thought that you were referring to whether the organization was best structured to deliver on strategy." Others nodded.

"I suspect that's what most people would have thought," Peter retorted. "Even some of the leading experts on organization design do not fully appreciate the central role of business processes. Anyone who has read the Goold and

Campbell HBR article that's on the reference list would know what I mean."

"In terms of my practical experience, I can't even begin to count the number of times I have sat with CEOs and observed the inclination to jump from a minor insight on a strategic issue to the need to somehow adjust the organization chart. This is not much better than rearranging the deck chairs on the Titanic."

"Even strong CEOs often don't seem to understand that the essential principle of business process design, driving organization design, is based on the simple and undeniable fact that a company creates value for its customers through the work activities that cross the boundaries of functional units or groups."

"As I maintain that organizations should be designed, led and managed in a way that makes it easy for the customer to do business with the company – and, equally important, makes it easy for employees to serve customers – then it follows that organizational alignment begins with the design of business processes, the clarity of measurement and the harmony of rewards – not fiddling with the organization chart."

"Okay, I think I'm really starting to get what you're driving at," Dave reflected. "I mean, our electrical manufacturing company tends to restructure every couple of years, and I've asked myself whether these reorganizations ever lead to any significant improvement in our performance. It's hard to tell. There are so many variables."

Peter amplified Dave's notion. "In my experience, that's par for the course. I think restructuring is one of the most frequently attempted, and poorly executed, of all business management activities."

"Why is that?" Dave asked.

"Well," Peter said, "there are several reasons."

"First, many executives still believe that if they can define the boxes on the organization chart right, and fill in the names of the 'right' people in the right boxes, then the organization's performance will 'automagically' improve. But this is rarely true."

"Second, organizations are not just *complex business systems*, as I said early on, they are equally complex *social* systems. So, because restructuring or reorganizing is one of the most visible kinds of change management, leaders are tempted to use restructuring as a universal hammer, where every problem looks like a nail."

"Third, reorganization looks like something that you can implement *fast*. You just announce it one week and the next week it looks like it's done – all the boxes have been moved around. The fact is, however, that it takes weeks or months for people to adapt to their new boxes. In the meantime, business performance often actually declines."

"But wait a minute," Fred asserted. "Isn't it a good thing for change management to be visible and fast to implement? There must be circumstances where it makes sense to reorganize."

"Yes, there are. Please understand," Peter explained, "organization structure is still important, for it affects the positioning of authority and the structure of reporting relationships, which, in turn, are important parts – but only parts – of that unique mix of values, strategic direction, performance measures and management incentives that go into organizational alignment."

"That's why I think – and this goes against the common wisdom, I admit – that there are two main reasons for changing an organization's structure: One is because the current structure is impeding the execution of strategy, and the other is because the current structure is affecting the performance of a critical business process."

"In addition, the only way I know of figuring out whether either of these is true is to examine the company's business processes in light of its strategic direction."

"I'll say it again. This requires a shared understanding by senior management of explicitly defined enterprise business processes, further effort such that the organization's core business processes are designed to deliver on its business goals, and more work to ensure that the organization design enables business process execution."

"And let's not forget, the details of the company's measurement and reward systems should be predicated upon an understanding of both business processes and structure."

Robin waggled her hand, and Peter motioned for her to go ahead. "Let's see if I'm on track here," she said. "You've said repeatedly that the behaviors driven by traditional functional thinking are problematic. Now you are saying that the traditional functional organization design is also a problem."

"That's right," Peter replied. "The traditional hierarchical, functional structure that has been popular for decades has a lot of staying power because it has proven answers to problems about economies of scale, standardization and specialization."

"In the past decade, though, critics are recognizing the way that this structure interferes with cross-functional communication. This is partly because both flexibility and speed have become such important characteristics of companies, given the rate at which customer and supplier needs are changing nowadays. If the cycle time for product or service development and the degree of responsiveness to customers is important to your business – as I think they are for every business – then your company is more likely to be moving away from the functional model toward alternative designs."

Fred jumped in, "That makes sense. What about the role of information systems?"

"Ahh," Peter said, "If we imagine the business process to be the train that delivers value to customers, then IT would represent the rails upon which the business process travels."

"Information technology is also an essential, enabling ingredient in alignment. The key concept here is that it's the assessment of business process performance that needs to drive development of IT systems – not the other way around."

"Some companies are beginning to explore the new BPM systems described as "the third wave" by Smith and Fingar to move the end-to-end business process, not the standalone functional application, center stage in business automation. Such an approach will not only help determine and design business processes, but promises to incorporate the needed measurements such as Six Sigma, directly into those processes, and provide the management 'dashboards' needed to monitor performance."

"I had an interesting off-line conversation with Bob yesterday afternoon. Do you have any comments, Bob?"

"Yes, I agree with the premise that business process performance needs to drive development of IT systems – not the other way around. But, in our organization, we're not there yet. The recent economic pressures are expanding the old "business – IT divide" into a virtual chasm."

"Amen to that," Lori said. "In theory, as the Director of Sales, I'm a customer of our IT department. In practice, I often feel like our sales organization is the IT department's pet guinea pig. In our company, we have gone through several iterations of so called 'sales force automation' and other CRM initiatives. While, I think we've finally got it right, it's taken three long and painful years."

A few people chucked, and Harry said, "My relationship with our IT people is not quite as discordant as Lori's. But, I must admit that I've had serious concerns regarding the payback from IT investments in our company. In the past, I'm embarrassed to admit that we have committed the sin of *automating broken business processes* more than once. When we worked on the 'dealer inquiry' process a couple of years ago, I found that I had to practically threaten our IT people with using outside consultants to get the intranet functionality we needed in a reasonable timeframe and with a reasonable investment. They finally did what we asked, but there were a few strong words exchanged. I am now a firm believer that IT investments need to be assessed based on the degree of operating improvement that they enable."

"Listening to Lori and Harry, I get the impression that we must be doing a few things right at our company," Bob said. "Of course, I'm a bit biased – since I'm in charge of

Information Systems. But we do try to understand both the cross-functional business processes that we intend to automate and the needs of the user community. This doesn't mean that we haven't had our challenges. As you probably know, most companies in the chemical sector have installed ERP or 'enterprise resource planning' systems. Our own implementation of our ERP system took far longer, and cost far more, than anyone had anticipated. More alarmingly, once we had completed the implementation, we realized that our business processes had changed but now they were cast in concrete in our ERP system!"

"I've gained two key insights over the past couple of years. First, the implementation of an ERP system does indeed involve the replacement of functional silos with more integrated, but nevertheless, 'enterprise silos.' We have really seen that with our ERP package and the challenges related to converting the systems of several small companies we have acquired over the past couple of years. Second, the Net – both the Internet and our intranet – have changed the rules of engagement for enabling systems development in ways we are just beginning to understand."

Bob was on a roll. He continued, "To build on Peter's comments, I believe that more and more business people are demanding that business processes be freed from their concrete castings. I'm excited by the possibility of separating the business process from our massive applications so that processes can be changed and managed without huge disruption and time delays. That's what we have wanted all along – the ability to adapt – and that need extends across the Internet to our trading partners."

"By the way, and to their credit, our ERP provider has *now* committed to a new platform it calls the 'process-tier' to drive business processes across different applications, technologies and organizations. We are in extensive discussions with our ERP provider about this new development. If we can get there from where we are now, it would really make a huge difference to the way we develop and operate our IT systems. It would help us to move beyond what we currently do, which is that we assess IT performance simply on the basis of projects delivered on schedule, on budget and planned functionality. We want to move a model that's based on measuring the *value* created for internal and external customers. Also, I think it would grease the wheels to get our executive team to step up to the bar on their accountabilities, much along the lines of the Ross and Weill HBR article we read last night."

"Thanks, Bob," Peter interjected. "This has been a fruitful discussion. Let's take a twenty-minute break. After the morning break, we'll work on a case study that will help reinforce some of the issues around alignment."

***

Fred grabbed a bottle of natural spring water. He walked over to where Peter was sitting and asked, "Are you up to answering a couple more questions on structure?"

Peter smiled, "Why not? Fire away."

Fred asked, "If organizations are indeed moving away from the traditional functional structure, what's your view on the direction of management thinking?"

"I've observed that management thinking on the topic of organization structure has evolved some," replied Peter. "Up until the seventies, most executives had a one-dimensional view of organization structure in terms of the traditional hierarchical organization. In the eighties, the matrix organization came into vogue, with a number of variants that adapted the model to variables like geography, product line, and so on. I'd call that a two-dimensional view of structure."

"Since the late nineties, though, you've got a number of powerful forces emerging, including consumer empowerment and the proverbial 'need for speed,' among others. I think this has encouraged three-dimensional thinking about organization structure. For example, you get companies starting to look at their organization in terms of product by market *and* geography, or market by geography *and* shared services."

"Interesting you should mention shared services," Fred interjected. "What's the business case for that model, as you see it?"

"I think it has a lot to do with a couple of things," Peter said. "On one hand, external forces are driving executives toward organizations built around market segments or product groupings. But they're worried that this way of doing business might lead to duplication of effort, such as developing redundant information systems, which, of course, would add to costs. And cost control is critical for just about any business these days, as you well know."

"To minimize this risk, executives are grouping key services such as finance, purchasing, information technology and legal in a shared-service organization. By so doing, they assure that all divisions will use the same information systems, the same chart of accounts and the same set of approved suppliers for purchasing. Clearly, these shared-services organizations offer benefits of scale, standardization and specialization."

"So it seems the trend is toward more complex organization structures," Fred said. "But doesn't that make it more difficult to communicate across organization boundaries?"

"Yes, it certainly can. That's precisely where the role of the cross-functional or cross-product group or cross-market teams becomes critical as does the alignment of policies and reward systems," Peter replied. "We know that human nature is such that once we bring together people in a group, people will develop deep loyalty to that group. Now, because most critical activities that involve serving customers cross organization boundaries, if we want people to focus on satisfying the needs of customers, as opposed to serving the needs of the group, we need to find ways to open the lines of communication across groups and assure that the focus is on satisfying customers. Cross-group teams and aligned reward systems, though not at all easy to achieve or implement, do just that."

"That makes a lot of sense," Fred said. "What about organizing along business process lines?"

Peter replied, "Let's see if we can tackle that one in the full group. We should get started soon."

Chapter 6: The Roll-Out

A few minutes later, once everyone was back, Peter got started. "This morning's case is designed to give you a sense of what is involved in the mid-level business process analysis that's needed to make decisions on alignment."

"It's based on the ROSECO Company, the regional office supply and equipment company we briefly considered yesterday. The case materials provide you with the leadership team's work at the enterprise level, and they also include mid-level draft documents, in swim-lane format, on the order fulfillment process."

"The case is designed to give you experience in asking the set of questions around business process, structure, measures, rewards and technology that need to be asked and answered in order to get the full picture on fit or alignment. Let's split into two teams to work on the case, and then we will reconvene to compare findings. How about Dave's side of the table going down to our breakout room, that's room number 102? Fred's side of the table can stay here. Questions anyone? All right, you have an hour and a half to prepare your solution to the case."

***

Once the group reconvened, both teams presented their solutions to the ROSECO case study. Then, Peter said, "Okay, I'd be interested in your views on what you liked about the case, and what you would have preferred to see differently."

Bob said, "I liked the case. ROSECO is an interesting company. I believe one of the reasons they've managed to survive intense competition from Staples and Office Max, for example, is because they have a pretty inspiring motto, 'Value beyond the product.' I also found the performance metrics around what constitutes a 'perfect order' to be useful, especially the fact that they measured on-time performance relative to delivering the product or service on the date when *the customer asked for it.* At our company, we are still in the mindset that customers have unreasonable expectations, so we stick to the old definition where on-time delivery means that we got it to the customer on the date that *we promised they would get it.* That's not really a crystal-clear example of a customer-centric metric, it's more like a safe company measure of performance."

Lori chimed in, "The case helped me understand the extent to which customer-touching processes such as order fulfillment are dependant upon certain support processes such as systems development and procurement. This leads to the other key insight I had from the case – which is that if you're looking at organizational alignment – you can't really talk about business processes without looking at the company's structure. The cross-functional or cross-group flow of activity is what really counts, and I'm beginning to see the pivotal role of the Process Owner."

Robin added, "I agree with Bob and Lori. However, I found the case information on rewards somewhat simplistic. I suppose it's okay to say that the rewards for executives at ROSECO need to be aligned with business process performance. After all, the case says they are rewarded according to a formula where 50% of their bonus is tied to company profitability and the balance is comprised of individual targets based on functional responsibility. So, now we propose that their VP Operations, the Director of Procurement, and the VP of the Call Center should have some part of their bonus based on the company's performance in fulfilling 'perfect orders.'

In our bank, executive compensation is clearly within the domain of Human Resources. They advise the CEO, who in turn takes the recommended package to the Board of Director's Compensation Committee. We just don't have the luxury of determining for ourselves the best set of formulas for rewards."

"You have a good point, Robin," Peter said. "You've put your finger on one reason why it's more difficult for standalone divisions of larger corporations to implement business process management, unless, of course, the entire enterprise is going down the same path. Nevertheless, I believe the ROSECO case surfaced the need for organizations to develop a reward system that creates shared accountability for closing key performance gaps. An aligned reward system needs to emphasize the company's key strategic themes. At ROSECO for example, it would be around customer satisfaction, growth and asset utilization."

Fred said, "There's another area where I would have liked to see a higher degree of complexity. I mean, we looked at the order fulfillment process. That was fairly straightforward, even though ROSECO fulfilled both product orders and service delivery. I would have been interested in exploring a more complex business process – new service development for example."

"I'll make a note of your point. However, let's recall that the amount of complexity we can handle in a case format is somewhat limited by the time available. But even more important the case reinforces the idea that we need to grapple with the complexity of BPM layer by layer. Enterprise business process analysis, to be effective, must defer the devil's details to lower-levels. At the enterprise level, we deal with the major inputs and outputs of major processes, and leave the detailed steps for further analysis, reconciling the two views along the way," Peter said.

"I have a couple of comments," Glen said. "By taking a mid-level look at the key steps and performance I can now start to imagine how this would be done for each enterprise business process with a key focus on the number of cross-functional hand offs and non-value-added steps. I can also see how this would identify the key process measures to be tied into the measurement system and provide data on any structural changes that may need to be made."

"Next, adding to what Bob said, I found the discussion on how ROSECO measures the Call Center's performance useful. In our mobile phone company, we still tend to measure things like 'average call handle time.' I believe that this type of measure drives the behavior of handling the call as quickly as possible, not necessarily to the best interest of customers. What we measure tends to drive human behavior and if we're not careful we may encourage our people to engage in behaviors that adversely affect customer service."

Peter said, "That's a good point, Glen. It's all too easy for companies to take an inside-out approach and fail to look at the business from the customer's point of view."

"I have a couple of questions," Jim said. "It appears that a mid-level review of business processes is a key factor in establishing organizational alignment. How is this done and how long does it take?"

"That's a tough one, Jim," Peter replied. "But I'll try to give you a general idea. The first thing to understand is that the decisions around alignment are arrived at iteratively. The mid-level business process review is meant to help the top team understand, in greater detail, the key steps, linkages and issues that exist with respect to the end-to-end enterprise business processes. It doesn't require maps that cover all the walls in the boardroom. Instead, it is best accomplished by a combination of high-level schematics, supported by summary charts."

"Let's take the ROSECO case as an example, since you just reviewed this case. ROSECO knows that promotion, sales, order fulfillment, service delivery, supply chain management and billing and collections are its key business processes. To conduct a thorough review, the Process Owners at ROSECO would need to form teams of middle managers and subject matter experts from across the key groups touched by each major process to look at the detailed steps involved. These teams would need to ask and answer many of the same questions you considered in the last case. What output does this process provide to customers? What do customers expect? How are we doing relative to customer expectations? What are the major steps, and handoffs in the process? What are the interdependencies with other business processes? What obvious implications are there for measurement, improvement, structure, rewards, technology, training, communication and so on?"

"If this work is done at the right level of detail, and assuming some intelligent pre-work, it takes anywhere from a couple of days to a week or so of concentrated effort. But the task does not end there. Once the details are fleshed out for each key business process, then it is possible to refine the high-level relationship map of how these business processes are linked to create value for customers and shareholders, and the role of supporting processes that enable the performance of the customer-touching business processes. This will take additional time to draft and validate with the executive team such that additional detail can be integrated with the high-level business process management and improvement plan. Iterative validation and integration is essential to *the rollout* of business process management. Does this answer your question, Jim?"

"Yes, it does," Jim replied. "It also leads me to my second question. What are the most important pitfalls to avoid in creating organizational alignment?"

"Well, the full answer could take a while, and we're approaching the lunch hour," Peter replied. "Let me just mention a few of the major pitfalls for now. The first, as we've discussed, is failing to have clarity on the assumptions around the external environment and the company's strategic direction – there's no substitute for that. The next major pitfall is failing to properly install process ownership and taking the time and effort to involve mid-level managers and providing them with the basic skills needed for process thinking. Then, if during the course of these activities, it becomes clear that there are one or two senior managers who are more concerned with protecting their turf than creating value for customers and shareholders, the third pitfall is failing to take prompt action on counseling or removing these executives. Next, there's the challenge of automating the collection of key business process performance measures. If this is not done well, the manual work involved will eventually sap the organization's energy. Equally significant can be the failure to integrate process performance in the management reward programs. Then there's the whole question of the executive's mindset around information technology. The pitfall to avoid is failing to change the way one thinks about the development and deployment of IT systems."

"In short, this is how I would describe the major pitfalls. However, let me emphasize again that if we look at the opposite side of the pitfall coin, we can see key opportunities. But, let's stop here for now and reconvene at quarter after one."

While the others were getting ready to leave for lunch, Dave approached Peter and said, "There's something I'd like to discuss with you. Would you be free to talk about it over lunch, or would you prefer that we talk at some other time?"

Peter replied, "Now would be fine, Dave. We can get a sandwich at the snack bar down the hall."

As they walked down the hall Dave began. "There's been talk of yet another restructuring at our firm and I thought I would pick your brains about applying your key concepts."

"No problem," Peter replied.

Once they were seated, armed with a sandwich and soda, Dave said, "I'd like to consider our firm's situation and get your reaction on alignment."

"Okay, Dave," replied Peter. "First, please tell me what is driving this talk of reorganization?"

"Well," Dave said, "it's our CEO who has raised the topic, but I suspect this is being driven by our Sales VP who seems to believe we're not structured to capitalize on market opportunities and respond to RFQ's."

"I see," Peter said. "Then, perhaps you would be kind enough to refresh my memory with an overview of the firm."

"Sure," Dave said. "Our company is a mid-sized manufacturer of custom-designed electrical systems for automotive transmissions. We serve both the heavy equipment and recreational vehicle industries, and have production plants in the US, Canada and off shore. Our strategic focus is to develop relationships with customers who value our internal engineering design capability, our ability to produce small runs of custom-designed equipment at competitive prices, and our responsiveness."

"That's fine," Peter commented. "Given your focus, what would you say are the major business processes for your firm?"

Dave answered, "We believe that our sales capability is the key to our success, so our sales process – and especially the quotation sub-process – is critical to our growth. Then, our materials management or supply chain and production processes are essential to keep our pricing competitive, and our engineering support process is an essential component in delivering on our promise to be responsive."

Peter thought for a moment, "Okay, that all sounds logical. What do you see as the company's key performance gaps?"

Dave said, "We've given that some thought. First, we need to improve the performance of the quotation process if we are going to meet our growth goals. Currently, it takes an average of 5 days to turn RFQ's around, and only 30%

of RFQ's received take advantage of our Web-enabled design capability or 'choice board.' We would like to see RFQ's turned around in 3 days and we believe that a key tactic in that regard is to have over 50% of RFQ's employ our 'choice board.' I should also point out that the group that receives RFQ's reports to the VP of Customer Service, and needs input from Engineering to respond to RFQ's, and then has to coordinate with Sales. Then, we have issues around our materials management process. We need to take action to reduce our cost of raw materials and improve our in-stock position for components. The Director of Procurement now reports to the VP Finance, but his primary focus is to provide materials for manufacturing. That's my department."

Peter made a couple of notes on his napkin. "OK Dave, so tell me more about how the firm is structured."

Dave smiled, "Well, currently we are set up in a sort of functional and market segment structure. As you know, I'm the VP Manufacturing, and we also have VP's in charge of Sales, Engineering, Finance and Customer Service. The Sales, Customer Service and Engineering departments are, in turn, organized by Market Segments such as heavy equipment, motor home, and so on. Now that I think of it, we have always had basically a functional structure and our reorganizations have revolved around taking a product or market segment focus."

"That's interesting," commented Peter. "An increasing number of companies are employing hybrid structures to take advantage of both economies of scale and to create responsiveness."

Dave said, "So tell me, Peter, what are your thoughts so far?"

Peter replied, "Okay, as long as we both appreciate that these comments are based more on my impression from what you have said as opposed to hard facts. On the surface, it sounds like your company has clarity on its strategic direction and knows what aspects of performance need to be improved. Certainly, there is nothing obvious, based on what you've said, which would indicate that the current structure could not work. Now, we can ask a few questions to get a preliminary sense for whether the organization is aligned to be able to deliver on those areas of performance improvement. As we just saw in the case study, alignment is not simply a matter of having the right structure – it also needs to include taking into consideration issues of performance measurement, business practices and policies and reward systems. I'd like to offer a few questions for you to consider, and a couple of suggestions that you may wish to discuss with your colleagues on the management team."

"In addition to the performance measure on RFQ turnaround cycle time, which appears to be in place, are there measures installed to monitor the amount of rework on RFQ's, the cost of raw materials as a percentage of sales per major order, the on-hand or out-of-stock performance for components?"

"Do you have a shared understanding of the inputs, key steps and outputs for these critical processes?"

"Do any of the indicators provide clues as to what might be the obstacles to improving performance? For example, are there any obvious reporting relationships that may increase the number of cross-functional handoffs for the key business processes you're considering?"

"In each case, is it possible to identify a senior manager who has a significant impact on his or her bonus, based on the performance of a key process such as RFQ turn around or Materials Management?"

"This last point is quite significant. While it's not part of the assigned reading in our workshop, Chapter 21 in Jack Welch's book, *Straight from the Gut*, outlines one example of the mental model needed to reward desired behavior. Welch put GE stock options where his mouth was – by making them available only to GE's certified Six Sigma *black belts*."

"Now, here are a couple of suggestions."

"Since there is no obvious evidence at this very high level to suggest that your current structure is standing in the way of executing strategy or impeding a critical business process' performance, it may make sense to look at it in more detail and focus on the degree of alignment of your policies, measures and rewards. So, whether you elect to install business process management, and all that entails, or not, you should at least spend some time talking about business process performance first, before you make any decisions on structure. You may find that useful."

"Also, there's a big difference between a wholesale restructuring and making some tactical structural changes, such as moving the reporting relationship of the group receiving RFQ's from Customer Service to Sales or moving the Procurement group from Finance to Manufacturing. The latter is far less disruptive and may get you eighty percent or more of what you're after, assuming that you fine tune measurement and reward systems."

David said, "You raise some very interesting points, Peter. Those questions will give me food for thought."

"Well, I suppose we both have to go and check voice mail. Thanks, I really appreciate the time you've spent with me today."

Chapter 7: Discipline

Once the group had reconvened after lunch, Peter began, "My sense is that you still have some questions and comments on the topic of alignment. So we'll begin with those. Then, I'll summarize this section, and we'll spend the balance of the day on the topic of Operating Discipline that includes an exercise on Business Process Ownership. Okay?"

People nodded.

"Then the floor is open for questions and comments," Peter said in a mock chairman's voice.

"If the Process Owners' roles are so essential, then as I mentioned to you during our morning break, I'd like to explore the risks and benefits of structuring along business process lines," Fred said.

"First, let me be clear on my bias," Peter replied. "I believe that we will see more and more companies structuring along business process lines. There are clear benefits in terms of the congruence of measurement, the potential for increased customer centricity, and the ability of articulating to employees how their contributions fit into the performance of the business as a whole. But it's not a panacea for all that ails a business. We have seen that managing cross-process linkages is just as important as managing cross-functional relationships."

"Let's say a company set up groups based on critical processes such as sales, order fulfillment, product development and supply chain. There would still be a need to establish cross-process communications to assure effective linkages across product development and sales, for example. This would be equally true for the linkage between supply chain and order fulfillment. Nevertheless, the process-managed organization can be the most effective alternative for companies where 'speed to market and responsiveness' are critical."

"Okay" Robin said, "But what about the fact that a lot of companies are moving toward smaller, more decentralized operating units?"

"You're right," Peter replied. "There are some companies such as Asea Brown & Bovari and Illinois Tool Works that are known for doing just that. There's a lot to be said for smaller operating units, especially if they can share common information systems for financial reporting and inventory control, human resource practices and things like that. It takes many of the complex structural issues out of the equation and provides people with a clearer sense of purpose and belonging."

Peter continued, "There are always alternative designs that might work for a given company. But whether they work or not has more to do with how successfully they align with strategy, and the effectiveness of the performance measures and reward systems they use, than with the structural model itself. And that's why I keep on saying that the *business process comes before structure and not vice versa.* In fact, the business process framework is the most effective way to model and test alternative organization structures. You have to discover what your critical business processes are and put the right metrics in place before you can even start to evaluate the effect of a particular organization design on your business in any meaningful way. And the new generation of business process management technology tools can radically simplify this process."

"One of my insights from the case yesterday and the one this morning was that your definition of business process management includes *improvement*. In fact, it could include the major redesign or reengineering of a critical process. So, I have a couple of questions," Glen said. "How does process improvement versus major reengineering fit with enterprise process management? What's the preferred approach, the do's, and the don'ts?"

"Whew, we could spend a lot of time on this one," Peter answered. "In the interest of time, I'll just hit the highlights. The decision to reengineer, or as I prefer to say, radically redesign a business process, should come out of the management team's work in tightly integrating business process thinking with strategy. It should be clearly identified as part of the business process management plan. It should not be a separate initiative. After all, the decision to radically redesign or incrementally improve a major business process is largely determined by the size of the gap between current and desired performance."

"As to the preferred approach, there seems to be a convergence of thinking on this topic. One needs simply to compare Rummler and Brache's chapter on redesigning business processes in the 1995 edition of their book on *Improving Performance* with Michael Hammer's 2001 article on the super-efficient company in HBR to see the parallels."

"It's interesting to note that Rummler and Brache have consistently maintained since 1991 that both process improvement and radical redesign involve many of the same steps. They talked about the steps of Project Definition,

Analysis, Design and Implementation and cautioned against 'throwing the baby out with the bath water.' In their view, the key differences in the approach are around the size of the performance gap to be bridged and the organization's appetite for change. Conversely, Hammer started out in the early nineties with only a radical 'big bang' approach. However, by 2001 Hammer's key steps of Scoping, Organizing, Redesigning and Implementing, which he cited in looking at cross-company business processes, have curiously come to resemble the steps outlined by Rummler and Brache."

"So, it's really not crucial what you call the change process. What's important is to be clear on the scope of change and charter the effort accordingly. This requires a team of people who do the work around redesign, often called a Design Team, and members of the executive team to steer and guide the effort, often called a Steering Team. In BPM, a cross section of enterprise process owners would sit on the Steering Team. They would work such that there's clarity of purpose, a deep commitment to change, a mechanism for ongoing dialogue between these teams, a dedication to employ a common technology and a continuing emphasis on communication. The pitfalls are legion, but the biggest ones are to be found in the early project structuring phase by not setting up the initiative properly, and the implementation stage where companies try to do too much too fast or are distracted from their original intent. Now, this has just touched on a few of the key points, Glen."

***

"Okay? Then, I propose to briefly wrap up the discussion on alignment and introduce the topic of operating discipline," Peter said, as he dimmed the lights at the front of the room.

"This morning we covered the fourth, fifth and sixth essential principles of business process management. The fourth principle stated that the firm's business processes need to be designed to deliver on its strategic objectives. We saw that this depends on the work done by the executive team in developing the enterprise-level business process management plan and in particular the size of the perceived gap between current performance and desired performance for each of the enterprise business processes. In alignment, the Process Owners have the key roles in chartering the needed cross-functional teams to analyze business process performance at a mid-level, and this data is essential in making decisions around organization design."

"Next, the fifth principle stated that organizations should be designed such that they enable business process execution and this is not simply a matter of structure. Instead, the leaders' thinking around organization design needs to encompass measures and rewards as well as structural issues."

"The final component of alignment is the continuing and even increasing role of how information technology is deployed. The sixth principle addresses this topic, and stresses that technology should be assessed, developed and implemented such that it enables business process performance – not the latest technology for technology's sake."

"It's the iterative application of these three principles that creates alignment or fit. It's the aggregate view on key sets of activities or capabilities to exploit market opportunity and lining up technology, structure, measures and rewards that creates a unique position in the marketplace and can lock out competitors."

Lori spoke up, "I know you said that the work around alignment is iterative. I'm sorry, but I still don't get it. These alignment issues are major decisions. I have visions of these teams going off to look at business process performance and I can't visualize how it all comes together."

"Excellent point," Peter said. "Do you see how the enterprise management plan developed by the executive team, in what we called strategic focus, can provide the initial guidance?"

"Yes," Lori said. "That details who owns which process and what degree of improvement is perceived to be needed."

"Fine," Peter continued. "Then, can you visualize how each Process Owner might form a process management team to look at his or her business process at a mid-level, and develop high-level recommendations around the key issues and opportunities, much as you did in the ROSECO case?"

Lori nodded her agreement.

"Then I'd suggest that it's the role of the executive team as the integrating body that may be the missing piece in the puzzle. Maybe I haven't emphasized that enough?"

Lori said, "That could be it. Could you say more about that?"

"Imagine a series of presentations by representatives of each business process management team to the executive team. Imagine that each presentation addresses the questions and makes recommendations on the topics you looked at in the ROSECO case. They talk about measures, rewards, structural issues, technology, training and communication. The executive team, which is really now functioning as a council of business process owners, listens and integrates this information to refine its enterprise-level view of business processes. Invariably, there are some conflicting views, and then the process owners go off line to resolve the issues. In the end, and let me restate that this is an iterative process, the business process management plan evolves to a more finite level of detail. Does that help?"

"I think so. I'll have to think about it some more," Lori replied.

Harry cut in and said," I thought I was on board this morning. Now, I'm feeling like a 'doubting Thomas' again. This sure sounds like a lot of work. I'm wondering, when are we ever going to find the time? In our company, we've made some good gains using Six Sigma. I'm not convinced that business process management will give us anything better than we got from Six Sigma."

"Good point, Harry," Peter replied. But before I get into it, let me ask the other participants, does everyone know what Six Sigma involves?"

Peter saw that there were a couple of blank stares. So he said, "Just for context, let's take a moment for a quick refresher on Six Sigma. The Greek letter SIGMA is a mathematical term that simply represents a measure of variation, the distribution or spread around the mean or average of any process or procedure. The term Six Sigma defines an optimum measurement of quality – no more than 3.4 defects per million events. Application of Six Sigma practice is targeted to reduce the variances in the product or business process."

"Six Sigma is a well-structured, data-driven method for eliminating defects, waste and other quality problems in manufacturing, service delivery, management and other business activities. It's been touted as a terrific way to improve performance by well respected firms such as GE, Allied Signal and others."

"So, let me get back to your question, Harry, by asking a couple of questions. How is your Six Sigma program set up?"

Harry said, "Each functional head has a number of Sponsors or Champions, master black belts and black belts. Most managers have been trained as green belts. Master black belts are coaches and black belts have an annual cost savings target to achieve."

"Thanks," Peter said. "So how much time was invested in training people in these various roles?"

"I'm starting get your point," Harry said. "That was a big hurdle for us to get over. Master black belts and black belts received several weeks of training, champions got a full week, and green belts received a 3-day training program."

"Now, would you say that you have deployed Six Sigma within an enterprise-wide framework? To test this, simply ask if the improvement projects address issues that cross broad organization boundaries or whether they tend to be more tactical within a department or specific group. Do you have an active Six Sigma Leadership council or Steering Committee? Is there a mix of large projects involving what's called design for six sigma or DFSS as well as the more typical improvement projects labeled with the acronym DMAIC, or define, measure, analyze, improve and control?"

"I'd have to say that we are taking more of a tactical approach," Harry said.

"Fine, yet it's working for you and that's great. But, you've invested significant time in Six Sigma training, and we haven't even talked about the effort involved in the DMAIC improvement projects. Further, you're not looking at the large cross-functional business processes, so chances are that you're leaving some big money on the table."

"Let's face it. Every major initiative takes time and effort. The difference with enterprise business process management is that your focus is on actually how the overall business works to create value as perceived by customers. If we don't have time for that, what do we have time for?"

Harry didn't say a word.

Peter continued, "I tend to believe that BPM is more robust than Six Sigma. It is a more flexible model, requires less advanced statistical knowledge, and can be used to more effectively pave the way for each person having at least as much allegiance to business process performance as to functional excellence. However, I think Six Sigma has a lot to offer. Unlike some other business process experts, I don't agree that Six Sigma has done for business performance what painting by numbers has done for the creative arts. In extremely large and complex organizations, Six Sigma should be a part of BPM, and it's important that the next generation BPM systems will have Six Sigma measures *built-in.*"

Peter paused for a moment to let this last remark sink in. Then, as he walked back toward the laptop, he said straight-faced, "Of course, you might say I'm prejudiced from my early experiences in observing large companies implement Six Sigma."

Even Harry smiled wryly at this.

***

Peter continued, "To get back to our knitting, so to speak, let me introduce the topic of Operating Discipline." "When I think of the business practices involved in Operating Discipline, I'm reminded of a quip attributed to Yogi Berra that says, 'In theory there is no difference between theory and practice. In practice there is!' We've seen that happen over the years with improvement initiatives such as TQM, reengineering, activity based costing and even with Six Sigma, as we discussed a moment ago. Enterprise business process management runs the same risk if we're not careful."

"In short, much of the work in establishing Strategic Focus and Organizational Alignment generally takes place at the senior management level. But getting the desired results requires that everyone in the organization be 'on the same page.' That's the essence of operating discipline."

"This leads to the seventh and eighth essential principles of enterprise management."

As the next slide appeared, he continued, "The seventh principle states that it's essential to 'hard wire' the enterprise measurement system to budgets and operating reviews. No surprise here, for as the old adage says, *what gets measured gets done.*"

"The eighth, and last principle, simply states that it's essential to maintain focus and alignment. This isn't easy. It requires constant communication, investing in people and technology and embracing change and innovation."

"I cannot overemphasize the role of constant communication. Leaders need to realize that BPM is first and foremost a different way of thinking and talking about the business. It's not a one-time event. Over forty years ago in his paper, *The Impact of Communications on Productivity,* William Oncken told the story of sagging productivity aboard a submarine.[2] It seems that even in times of war, productivity can sag. When people are not necessarily doing what they are supposed to do, the boilers do not produce quite enough steam. The problem aboard the sub was that the folks in the bowels of the ship were not kept informed of their position, where the enemy was, or where they were going. The solution was simply to turn on the microphone of the guy with the periscope. The public address system gave the entire ship a running account of what was on the horizon and the plan of attack. Suddenly, the boilers were at full steam."

"People want to know. We are 'explaining' creatures. The need for explanation and constant communication is a fundamental part of the human condition. In the battles for the 21st century marketplace, people need to be constantly *in-the-know*, not just fed a one-time vision statement."

"Let's also recognize that companies that have a catchy and compelling vision statement will be better positioned to clearly communicate everyone's role in 'the way ahead' versus those that don't. For example, ROSECO's vision of 'Value beyond the Product' lends itself well to be the inspiration in helping everyone to understand their role. If the leadership team at ROSECO frames each of the critical business processes in light of 'value beyond product' then it's not too great a leap to figure out what order takers, order makers, order shippers and service providers need to do to make this vision a reality."

"What about those companies that don't have such an inspiring vision statement?" asked Lori.

"Well, even a dull, generic vision statement can be leveraged. I know of a contract manufacturing company in your industry, the pharmaceutical industry. Their vision statement says 'We will become the Contract Manufacturer of choice by exceeding our customers' requirements through providing a compliant range of products, regulatory support and supply chain services.' Boring? Maybe. Generic? Certainly. Yet it's proven to be useable, nevertheless, when frequently communicated in combination with clarity on the key business processes, strategic initiatives and a congruent perspective on performance measures, rewards and information technology."

Fred said, "So if I understand correctly, a fundamental aspect of maintaining operating discipline requires that the key elements of strategic direction be communicated regularly, that the company's measurement system be used to monitor progress toward strategic goals and that a business process framework be employed to communicate to each employee their prospective role in this regard."

"Yes, that's it so far, but it doesn't stop there. An additional essential element is to monitor the *external environment* and conduct a regular review of strategic direction. Given the level of turbulence in most market segments, the days of the strategy being limited to the annual strategic retreat are long gone."

"Management luminary Peter Drucker noted in *Management Challenges of the 21st Century*,[3] that executives need to organize and manage, not only the cost chain, but also everything else – including strategy and product planning – as one economic whole, *regardless of the legal boundaries of individual companies.*" In short, information outside the company is just as, if not more, vital than what's going on inside the company. This requires peripheral vision, not just myopic internal focus."

"Some companies create advisory boards comprised of both internal and external people including marketing staff, industry experts and others to monitor competitive and technological trends and report to the leadership team. Other companies regularly convene a group of known internal contrarians simply to challenge the thinking of the top team. Whatever the tactic, the desired result is to have a mechanism that can anticipate changes in the competitive environment."

"The next element of operating discipline is to create a climate or culture where each person internalizes the goals of the business process within which they work and his or her individual contribution. This generally involves an investment in training people on business process thinking and requires common language and a clear definition of the major business processes including where the process starts, where it ends, what's the output, who's the customer, how performance will be measured and what are the key process steps."

"Typically, three levels of training are needed. Senior management needs to have a shared understanding of the BPM principles, their major business processes and their linkages. This should be developed during the senior management team's work on Strategic Focus and Organizational Alignment. Middle management needs to have the same understanding – but should also be trained in the methods to improve and manage business processes. Finally everyone in the organization requires BPM awareness training."

"It should be clear by now that individual Process Owners need to provide tactical leadership. So, let me share with you my views on the behavioral aspects of Process Ownership that reflect the some of the practical challenges in implementing BPM. This will probably take a few minutes, and will serve to stimulate your thinking with respect to the team exercise this afternoon on the same topic."

"As a starting point, let's recognize that leaders who wish to employ BPM need to expect that some shift in the executive team's perceptions or mental models will be required. The degree of success in day-to-day operations is largely determined by how Process Ownership is practiced at the senior management level, for Process Owners have overall accountability for monitoring; addressing and solving critical issues in their cross-functional, enterprise business process."

"Some of the key challenges process owners face include: maintaining customer focus, automating process performance measurement, promoting the needs of customers and process performance without threatening other functional leaders, and engaging the support of all employees affected by the business process."

"To address these challenges, process owners need to behave differently. As some of us observe daily, many senior managers grew up within a 'command and control' environment, where questions such as 'What is the scope of my responsibility?' 'What tasks must I execute?' and 'Who are the key subordinates who can help me look good?' were foremost and top of mind."

"In making the transition to BPM, Process Owners need to promote the shift in perception from the traditional view where the dominant factors are reporting relationships and flow of authority, to a more customer-centric and business-process focused paradigm. In this transition, the factors that dominate the process owner's thinking are the products and services provided to customers (external and internal), the flow of value-added work, and relevant roles and responsibilities."

"This involves more than paying lip service to customer needs. It requires not only a mechanism to assess the timeliness, quality and cost of products and services provided to customers, but also a different set of supporting documentation, measures and decision-making mechanisms than those that are traditionally the norm."

"In this context, the supporting documentation to enable performance measurement, problem solving and decision making assumes a new shape. The emphasis shifts from procedure documentation and linear mapping of workflow to a more comprehensive cross-functional view that not only specifies who does what, but also the key points of leverage in providing the necessary products and services."

"This shift in thinking has major repercussions. It means having the ability to manage through influence as opposed to control – by looking at areas under direct control, as well as the areas not under direct control. Hammer makes this point forcefully in his 1999 HBR article you read last night."

"The documentation of the complex cross-functional set of business processes is essential to establish clarity around the degree of interdependence, the identification of an appropriate set of performance measures and finding the key leverage points for performance improvement. It not only creates a tangible document that facilitates a more adaptive view of the business, stressing the interdependencies, but it's also a terrific communication vehicle for fact-based discussions with peers in resolving key issues. Such fact-based discussions are made even more plausible with the metrics and simulation facilities built into some of the new BPM systems."

"Goal setting also requires a different perspective. Traditionally, authority and responsibility are defined by functional, cost center, or profit center parameters and the focus is on individual managers delegating parts of their responsibilities in a one-on-one setting. In contrast, process owners should stress the shared or joint responsibility for providing clearly defined services to customers and focus on the results achieved by the team of managers responsible for the end-to-end flow of work."

"This shift in thinking with respect to goal setting has direct implications for how resources are allocated and budgeted. In a traditional system, individual operating units make their case for resources on the basis of their own unit's requirements. Conversely, process owners are more likely to work with the team of managers who are responsible for delivering services to customers. They would jointly develop a case for resources based on the integrated flow of work – the end-to-end business process – that creates and delivers value for customers."

"This end-to-end process mode of thinking cascades into how performance is measured. With this approach, there is often a shift away from the traditional focus on "actual versus budget" line item performance for individual units. Instead, performance measures are focused on the quality, timeliness, and cost of products and services provided to customers."

"These requirements can present a major challenge in terms of the development of automated means to gather performance measures. In many traditional organizations, the development of information systems evolved within functional silos, where the information needs of downstream departments were considered only on a secondary basis – if at all. Automating horizontal, fact-based performance measures in this type of environment is challenging at the best of times."

"In traditional organizations, problem solving is all too often compromised by lack of a common goal. Periodically, individual unit managers compete with and confront one another and senior managers often need to arbitrate or intervene in decisions several levels down in their organizations. In business process managed organizations, process owners are clearer on common goals. They are sensitive to departmental interdependence needed for issue resolution and are more likely to conduct cross-group problem solving sessions within the context of providing services to customers and the required flow of work."

"The success of such sessions of course depends on having a common view of the process, fact-based data on desired and actual performance and the interpersonal skills to influence peers. In many cases, the performance measures provided for end-to-end business process reveals where actual performance has fallen in sub-processes, making it obvious to all where improvement is needed. With such BPM performance information available, the data does the influencing on peers!"

"Cross-group analysis and problem-solving sessions can have a major impact on the way in which decisions are actually made. Contrary to the "command and control" tradition, where senior managers sometimes guarded their "big picture" view and their right to the ultimate responsibility for key decisions, process owners are more likely to encourage group decision making. Group decision making doesn't make decisions any easier, but the approach means that those affected by decisions are indeed the ones who took part in making the decisions – building in incentives to execute once decisions are made. The transition to group decision making is not an abdication of responsibility by process owners; instead it's a necessary consequence of recognizing the extent to which operating units are interdependent in providing products and services."

"Once process owners acquire a more comprehensive view of cross-functional performance, they will often tend to encourage problem solving and decision making as close to the front line as possible. This frequently leads to a shift toward team-based organizations, and process owners become coaches with their jobs on the line if they don't create winning teams. This trend also reinforces why I assert that BPM is a team sport."

"So what changes as senior managers become process owners and embrace process management?"

"The key changes are related to a systemic view of the business and an appreciation for the complexity and interdependence involved in providing outstanding value to the firm's customers."

"In a nutshell, that's my view of the thought model changes and the key challenges for process owners," Peter concluded.

Bob said, "Don't you think that's pretty optimistic? I'm just thinking about our executive team, and I'm not sure that even half of our senior people have the capacity to make that type of transition."

"Unfortunately, that's about right," Peter said somberly. "I've observed that anywhere from a quarter to half of executives in a firm that embraces enterprise management will either leave or be asked to leave within a year of the effort being launched."

No one said a word.

***

Peter continued, "Now, to further deepen our understanding of Process Ownership, I propose we explore two key topics relating to operating discipline in break out groups which will tie in last evening's reading assignments. Let's keep the same teams as yesterday, and please take reprints of the reading assignments from the back table if you need them. For the team on Dave's side of the table, I'd like you to discuss the role of Process Ownership in Operating Discipline. The team on Fred's side of the table is asked to discuss the benefits and risks of improving cross-company, end-to-end business processes. Please take an hour and a half to develop your views, refer to the reading materials and, of course, draw on your own experience."

Ninety minutes later, the group reconvened. Peter said, "Let's begin with the discussion on the notion of Process Ownership."

Dave stood up to represent his team. "We agreed that Business Process Ownership is the key tactic for assuring accountability for business process results. This requires creating the means by which people will become comfortable asking meaningful questions on business process performance, and working to make sure that people have at least as much allegiance to business process performance as to their functional roles. We see that perspective as a major, major change in thinking."

"Ideally, we see several levels of Process Ownership for optimal, sustainable performance. First, it makes sense that each member of the executive team be accountable for the performance of an end-to-end, business-critical process. At this level, the Process Owner should be the executive who has most at stake, based on the performance of that business process."

"The executive Process Owner needs to monitor the performance of the process, ensure that the business process measures tie into the organization's performance measures, make certain that individual and team rewards reinforce and support improved business process performance, and keep an eye on evolving technology that can be employed to enable performance improvements. Also, the Process Owner needs to select the members for a standing process team and chair regular meetings."

"We feel that the selection of the process team members by the executive Process Owner is crucial. Each member should own a discrete part of the process. For example, the executive process owner for an order fulfillment process may dissect the process into the discrete sub-processes or capabilities of order taking, order picking, order shipping, billing and inquiry handling. In this way, the standing process team would be comprised of representatives from different functions or groups and each member would in turn own their part of the process."

"We do not support the position that business process ownership can be assigned as a staff responsibility. We simply don't see how this approach will drive the needed allegiance to business process performance. It requires executive commitment."

"Further, management of *cross-company* business processes represents an exceptional challenge! When you consider that an average end-to-end business process that delivers ultimate value to customers crosses company boundaries and consists of multiple participants, how do we address the notion of process ownership in that context? The lessons from exemplar performers such as Boeing, Dell Computer, GE and Cisco lead us to believe that it requires executive commitment, metrics across the value chain, shared inter-company rewards and a deep dedication to serving the ultimate customer."

"With cross-company business processes, the challenge of team building goes to new heights. We have all observed that when it comes to major league sports, overall team performance is a far more critical to winning than any one player's individual performance. We think that companies should keep in mind the concept of team performance as they form multi-company teams to build end-to-end business processes – just one more reason for leaders to appreciate your point, Peter, that business process management is a team sport!"

"That captures the key points. Are there any questions?"

Lori asked, "Did you discuss the possibility that the heads of functional groups would be threatened by the Process Owners?"

"Yes, we did," Dave answered. "Our view is that if the activities in Strategic Focus and Organizational Alignment are properly executed then there would be a shared understanding by the members of the executive team on the crucial role of business process management. Assuming that there are supportive executive reward systems, we felt that there should be relatively low levels of conflict between the heads of the functional areas and the process owners. Of course, that's in theory, and it may be different in practice. The most likely area of conflict would be around resources – and that's actually healthy since it would really test the leadership team's commitment to BPM."

"Thanks Dave," Peter said. "Let's hear what the other group developed with respect to the benefits and risks of improving cross-company business processes."

Lori said, "We had a pretty lively discussion on this topic. To begin with, we decided that cross-company, end-to-end process improvement and management is simply not possible without first being in command of key processes internally. An organization needs to have had a certain degree of success with internal process improvement, enterprise BPM, and have key elements of business process thinking installed in its culture before embarking on cross-company ventures."

"However, given certain circumstances, there are significant benefits to looking at major business processes such as supply chain across companies. For example, the procurement process is largely a mirror image of the supplier's sales and order fulfillment process."

"Jim and Glen provided examples from their businesses of how the improvement of a cross-company business process could yield big results. High-speed Internet service providers typically use large quantities of cable modems and they subsidize the costs to consumers. The same holds true in the cellular phone industry, where the sale of mobile handsets is typically subsidized and large volumes are involved."

"We feel that once an opportunity is identified, the next thing to check is whether there is a compatible level of business process thinking within supply-chain partners."

"However, we felt cross-company business process ownership brings into play certain cultural factors and probably involves greater levels of complexity than what Dave just described."

"Now, getting back to the key steps in streamlining one or several cross-company business processes, we discussed a number of critical factors. We felt that the business process of each company, along with the underlying data for those processes, must be synchronized in real time whenever possible. This mode of operations is crucial, for information latency blocks visibility across the value chain. We discussed that the new generation of BPM technologies may open major new possibilities for real-time interactions between and among trading partners that could actually redefine competitive advantage in many industries."

"Here are the key points summarizing our discussion. Cross-company streamlining efforts have to be tied to the strategic interests of all companies involved. The effort needs to involve the right people, in the right way, especially senior managers – from all participating organizations – and the early involvement of IT people is essential. Cross-company process teams need to be given a clear charter, and speed is vitally important. The senior managers from the companies need to agree that it's not necessary to blow up the current business process. With cross-company efforts, senior management needs to be even more vigilant in considering how the changes will affect the people touched by the process all the way across the value chain."

"In certain industries, managing cross-company business processes is simply not an option – it's a requirement. Consider the impact that the 800-pound gorilla, Wal-Mart, has had in the retail sector with its leadership in vendor-managed inventories. Participants in this sector simply can't afford to ignore the potential efficiencies in managing the supply chain across company boundaries. They are told to, and they do – full stop."

"Now, we'd be pleased to respond to any questions."

Robin said," Did you talk about the impact of a cross-company business process improvement effort on process ownership?"

"As a matter of fact, we did," Lori replied. "Jim, given that you had some pretty firm views, maybe you would like to respond to this one?"

"Sure," Jim said. "I brought up the example of cable modems in our high speed Internet business. Over 85% of the cable modems we use are from one supplier. It would make a lot of sense to look at the entire supply chain from the supplier's factory right through to the successful installation of the cable modem in the customer's home. Cross-company cultural issues then become crucial. The initiative would work best if our supplier had a Process Owner for the Sales Process and the Order Fulfillment process, and we had a Process Owner for the Purchasing Process and the Service Delivery and Installation Process. Then, these Process Owners would form the executive steering team for the initiative."

"If the supplier and our own company had dramatically different levels of business process maturity, we would have to close the gap with process education and training. We would need to test our respective views and practices with respect to BPM prior to entering into a new way of managing the end-to-end process."

"Next, we would need to measure the performance of the entire cross-company business process and make sure that there are meaningful inter-company rewards for Process Owners and key managers, and the profit-risk sharing of the companies as a whole. For example, when the strong demand for Internet routers fell from the sky with the dotcom crash, I've heard that Cisco apparently assumed a $2-billion inventory write off rather than dump the loss back onto its contract manufacturers – sometimes it's not just profits, but also losses that get shared!"

"Thank you, Lori and Jim," Peter said. "If there are no further questions, let me briefly summarize this section and talk about our agenda for tomorrow and the reading assignments for this evening."

***

"This afternoon, we have seen that the Process Owners' role is critical in terms of installing greater discipline in daily operations. Process Owners are accountable for cascading business process thinking throughout the organization – and across the value chain to trading partners. Process thinking is best accomplished via the creation and nurturing of business process management teams and the tight linkage of business process performance measurement to operating reviews. The activities needed to sustain focus and alignment require a fundamental shift in the mindset of the firm's leaders, a dedication to embrace continuous change, and investments in people and technology."

***

"In the morning, we'll begin with an open discussion to address any outstanding issues or questions. Then, we'll spend the balance of the morning in working on a comprehensive case study. In the afternoon, I'll summarize the program and there will be time set aside for each of you to develop your personal action plan."

"Here's the reading assignment for this evening."

Reading Assignment

The Audio-Tech Executive Book Summary of Larry Bossidy's and Ram Charan's *Execution* and

John Kotter's "Leading Change: Why Transformation Efforts Fail," from the March-April 1995 edition of the *Harvard Business Review*.

As Bob and Glen walked across the hotel parking lot toward their cars, Bob said, "It's finally starting to come together."

"Ditto," Glen replied. "The more I think of it, the more I'm convinced that business process innovation is largely a matter of leadership."

"It sure is," Bob said. "I mean BPM requires crystal clarity on the purpose for the business, but once established, leaders can use the framework to really create context and to establish a sense of urgency around the firm's critical business issues and drive action at several levels throughout the organization."

"Agreed," Glen said. "But it goes beyond that. Process owners really have to be good at navigating past obstacles."

"Yes, and I can see how that may involve transferring or dismissing members of the team who visibly do not support the statement of purpose and the overall change agenda, or simply coaching others to focus on the critical priorities for change," Bob said.

"Also, BPM reinforces the need for executives to communicate persistently. To take advantage of every opportunity to reinforce the vision, emphasize the need for urgency, to describe what's at stake, and what results must be achieved by when. If that's not leadership, I don't know what is," Glen added. "Leadership isn't a platitude, it's one hell of a lot of work."

"Hey, we're starting to sound like Peter," Bob said, with a chuckle. "Good thing that tomorrow is the last day of the workshop. These new ideas are intense and I could use a little rest to digest them."

"Yeah," Glen said. "Well I'm going home to test out my leadership on the terrible teens. See you in the morning."

Chapter 8: The Wrap Up

Bob was running a bit late this morning. Everyone else was seated by the time he got to the meeting room. He fetched a cup of coffee, sat down beside Glen and said, "So, are you ready to execute?"

"Yeah, I'm just about ready to execute some of my colleagues in Marketing," Glen said. "Those guys drive me nuts. Just when the network is beginning to stabilize, they introduce a promotional program offering unlimited night-time minutes – without telling us. Well, due to the peak in volume, we had all kinds of dropped calls last night, and it got so bad that the problem escalation even reached me. Can you believe that? Nowhere to hide!"

"Sure can," Bob said. "Problem escalation procedures are great, as long as it's during business hours. Right?"

"Yeah," Glen grimaced.

Just then, they noticed that Peter was about ready to kick off the morning session. "Good morning – once again. So, this is it, the last day of our workshop. Today's agenda is about putting it all together. The theme is 'how to get it done' or as the Nike commercial used to say, *Just do it.*"

"I'd like to say a few words about maintaining focus and alignment and then have an open discussion on any outstanding items you may wish to explore. Then, I'll provide a recap of the course content as a lead up to the major case study that will serve to pull everything together. Completion of the case study will take several hours, and I propose that we work through lunch. After the case debrief, which should take us to mid afternoon, you'll have the opportunity to develop your individual action plans. Of course I'll be available to respond to any questions you may have in this regard."

"As discussed yesterday, the two essential principles in operating discipline involve tightly linking business process performance measures to budgets and operating reviews, and sustaining focus and alignment."

"While it takes considerable effort to set up the BPM framework; that scope of effort pales in comparison to what is needed in order to sustain focus and alignment. Installing and maintaining enterprise-wide business process management is largely a matter of leadership."

"Fortunately, BPM provides leaders with a number of powerful conceptual and practical ways to sustain momentum. Last night's reading assignment provided you with the opportunity to review Kotter's 'Eight Stage Model of Creating Major Change' and Bossidy and Charan's work on the 'The Leader's Seven Essential Behaviors.' Just consider how business process thinking fits in with some of the concepts in those articles."

"Imagine how leaders can establish and maintain a sense of urgency by relentlessly defining the gap between current and desired business process performance. Consider the potential of creating a guiding coalition through the team of senior leaders acting as the firm's process owners. Can you see how the rollout of business process management can contribute to empowering broad-based action and serve to generate short-term wins? Envision how the BPM framework equips leaders to insist on realism, set clear goals and priorities, and supports leaders' ability to follow through. Consider how the BPM framework provides leaders with the means to communicate with employees in more relevant and meaningful terms. Recall that sustaining focus and alignment requires that leaders consciously and persistently invest in people and technology."

"I challenge you to consider these thoughts as you work through the case later today. So, given this introduction, let's move on to any questions you may have now."

Robin said, "You just mentioned investing in technology, and I know we talked about this yesterday, but I'm interested in getting more clarity on how BPM will work to put technology in the proper context for providing customers and suppliers with better information, and employees with the means to do their work faster, better and cheaper."

"All right," Peter said. "Here are my thoughts, and then maybe others may want to add to them. The BPM thought model encourages leaders to deploy appropriate process-oriented technology as a solution to the critical issues that the firm faces. The high-level analysis of the enterprise surfaces questions such as: Which business processes need to be significantly improved through the deployment of information technology? What results might we expect? What is the best sequence for deploying enabling technology? Then, the mid-level analysis raises questions such as: How many concurrent projects can the organization sustain with the new process-oriented technology as compared to the older functional application-oriented approach?"

"You will appreciate that this line of thinking is significantly different from what happens within organizations that are managed according to traditional functional lines. In traditionally managed companies, the responsibility for developing an IT strategy is often delegated to the senior IT executive and the IT staff. Since the IT specialists are often more knowledgeable about technology than they are about the business, this can result in a lack of clarity on the business benefits of IT initiatives and can also result in the proliferation of IT projects. So, it's no surprise that there's a lot of finger-pointing at the IT department when projects don't deliver on time or to expectations."

"That's my snapshot view," Peter concluded. "Anyone else want to take a crack at answering Robin's question?"

"Yes, I'd like to add to that," Bob said. "While the exact technology solutions are unique to each company and situation, I believe that BPM increases the chances that the leadership team will take accountability for IT investments. As Peter implied, this occurs because in the BPM approach, the technology issues are surfaced iteratively as the leadership team develops an understanding of the performance, and the key gaps in the execution of key business processes. So, if this iterative approach is used, then senior management should acquire a very clear sense of where technology will enable performance and can make more informed decisions on which IT projects should be funded, what results can be expected and what the likely payback might be."

"On the technical side, we should note the opportunity that the new category of BPM software affords. Unlike the massive, expensive and disruptive "conversions" characteristic of large ERP systems, the new breed of BPM systems exploit a firm's existing information systems and can be implemented incrementally, one business process at a time. This approach may result in getting to the point where the return on process investment (ROPI) will likewise be incremental, facilitating risk management."

"Thanks, Bob," Peter said. "There's just one thing I'd like to add. The corporate community should firmly encourage IT vendors to accelerate their efforts in developing this technology, and finally provide their customers with what they've needed all along."

"What about the trend of outsourcing IT services?" Lori asked.

"That's a very relevant question," Peter replied. "There has been an increasing trend to outsource IT services, driven in part by the complexity of implementing and maintaining ERP systems. Now that Web-based IT solutions are becoming increasingly critical, this trend may well continue, since many traditional IT departments may not have the needed depth of expertise in the Internet arena. I believe this is essentially the approach Borders Books took when it outsourced its entire Internet operations to Amazon."

"Whether IT services are outsourced or not is a fundamental business decision that management needs to make based on what they see as the firm's core business and how IT fits in. What's important is that the leadership team must not abdicate its accountability and responsibility for enabling technology. They must make the key decisions on how much to spend on business process automation and management and where to apply enabling BPM technology for what operating results."

"What's really new here is not just IT outsourcing, for that's been done for some time now. It's the new potential to outsource business processes with the necessary transparency, accountability and control that's beginning to catch the attention of a growing number of companies. Some experts believe that BPM and its associated technologies may make business process outsourcing or BPO one of the most fruitful means to cut costs, gain new capabilities and make course corrections as markets and economic conditions change – as they always will."

Jim said, "I've got a question on a different topic. We haven't talked much about culture. What are your thoughts on aligning culture?"

"There's been a lot written on culture," Peter said. "But over two decades of consulting, I've got to confess that organization culture is one of the most amorphous and difficult areas to tackle. Frankly, most companies struggle with identifying the key determinants of culture. Clearly, the quality of leadership is one major factor that impacts organization culture – especially as it directly influences the clarity of purpose and the degree of openness, decisiveness and energy in the organization. Some of the other key factors I've noted include the nature of the reward systems, the extent of empowerment and the degree of congruence between stated values and actual behavior."

"Few would argue that a robust organization culture demands clarity of purpose and clear goals and priorities. This is the task of the leader. But, this is just the beginning. In addition, a vibrant culture requires honest dialogue and realism in terms of the key performance gaps the company faces and its plans to close these gaps. The BPM approach provides a mechanism to establish the set of performance reviews that can serve as the framework for such dialogue at the executive team level. Then, this needs to be replicated at several levels throughout the organization through meetings, follow-up and feedback. Anyone wish to add, change or delete what I've said?"

"I just want to underline that the role of rewards is crucial," Glen asserted. "In thinking about this last night, I concluded that a solid culture is built on a set of rewards that are simultaneously balanced and consistent. Balance is achieved by having reward systems designed with a view to organizational, business process and functional performance, such that maximum rewards are earned if targets are achieved in all three areas, but some rewards may be realized by people with outstanding performance in the latter two categories – even if the overall organizational targets are not achieved. I believe that consistency is equally critical. As Bossidy and Charan point out in the reading assignment article, outstanding performance should trigger generous rewards. If the focus is on teamwork, then an aspect of the reward system should be based on team rewards and not *just* individual bonuses."

Bob added, "I think that an organization's typical reaction to mistakes is just as important. I know because I've made my share. I'd argue that the most energetic cultures are characterized by a profound understanding that assertive action necessarily involves making mistakes which are points of learning and not a basis for reprimand."

"Thanks, Glen. Thanks Bob. Those are good additions," Peter said. "Just one more point and we'll leave the questions of culture. See what you started, Jim?"

"I'd suggest that the degree of congruence between stated values and actual behavior will also give us insights on the viability of an organization's culture. A dynamic culture is characterized by a high degree of congruence in this respect. If there is a dedication to addressing key aspects of performance with urgency, then executives act accordingly.

If an organization is committed to being the low cost producer in the industry, then the look and feel of the executive offices should reflect just that. If the organization is intent on being number one in its industry, then the will to win must be evident throughout the organization. If the organization is dedicated to being nimble and quick, then its hierarchy should be relatively flat and reflect those values. If an organization has a stated value of egalitarian ethics, then that calls for a broad-based stock option program and argues against executive parking spaces, executive washrooms or dining rooms, nor lavish corner offices," Peter said.

"Well, I'm not quite done yet," Jim said. "Now that we've opened this can of worms, I'm interested in your thoughts on the key pitfalls to avoid in developing a culture that supports BPM."

"Okay," Peter said. "Let's begin with the premise that business process management is a team sport. So, to turn your question around just a bit, let me briefly mention what I see as three of the major cultural challenges that can stand in the way of leaders implementing BPM. The first of these is a climate of indecision, characterized by failure to make the *tough* decisions, lack of open, honest dialogue and inconsistent follow-up and follow-through. That's a tough obstacle for any team to overcome. The second challenge is a lack of openness to change, often visible as a mechanical adherence to precedence. I've seen that in a few conventional companies where tradition is revered, product development cycle times are long and profit margins are slim, yet consistent. Finally, let's understand that a culture of what I call 'cowboy' behavior that encourages risk taking without accountability, can be equally daunting to overcome."

Peter glanced at the clock, and said, "In the interest of the time remaining, let's move on to the course recap, which leads in to this session's major case."
Peter took a minute to get set up, and projected the now familiar slide of the eight essential principles.

1. Look at the business from the *outside-in,* from the customer's perspective, as well as from the *inside-out.*
2. Tightly integrate strategy with enterprise business processes.
3. Articulate strategy to inspire, from the boardroom to the lunchroom.
4. Design enterprise business processes to deliver on strategic goals.
5. Ensure that organization design enables enterprise business process execution.
6. Deploy enabling technology based on the value added to enterprise business process performance.
7. Hard wire the enterprise performance measurement system to budgets and operating reviews.
8. Sustain focus and alignment

Then, he said, "As you know, my claim is that enterprise management is a team sport. You've got to want to win, and this requires that cross-functional or cross-group teams work together to create value for customers and shareholders. When well executed, business process management facilitates greater clarity on strategic direction, alignment of the organization's resources to support strategy implementation, and a higher degree of discipline in daily operations.

My terms for these results are strategic focus, organizational alignment and operating discipline. Further, we've discussed eight essential principles that are the foundation of implementing business process management."

"To review these eight principles it's helpful to ask three key questions about each. Why do it? What are the key steps? What are a few of the major pitfalls to avoid?"

1) "The first essential principle is to look at the business from the *outside-in*, from the customer's perspective, as well as the *inside-out*. Why do it? To be successful, companies must explicitly understand and measure what customers require and the extent to which current business process performance meets customer and company requirements. The key steps involve first expressing customer requirements, typically in terms of value, quality and timeliness. Next, we need to explicitly define the enterprise business processes to gain clarity around the inputs, outputs, major sub-steps, functions involved for each. We'll also establish the performance measures for those processes, typically in terms of various attributes around quality, time, cost and productivity. Then, we need to assess current business process performance in terms of the previously mentioned measures from both a customer and a company point of view."

"There are two major pitfalls in applying this principle. The first is a lack of honesty and courage in measuring what really counts. I recall that Bob provided us with a good example when he mentioned that some managers believe that customers are unreasonable, and so it's more meaningful to measure the variance to promised date in order delivery, as opposed to the variance to requested date. The fact that customers are increasingly demanding, as Robert Rodin argues in his 1991 book, *Fast, Perfect, and Now*, is no reason not to measure how you're doing relative to their requirements. The second pitfall is working at the wrong level, diving into too much detail too soon. It's important to gain clarity on enterprise performance before diving into further details."

2) "The second essential principle states that the company's strategy needs to be tightly integrated with business process management. Why? This is where the rubber hits the sky. The undeniable, simple truth is that work gets done through cross-functional business processes. So articulating strategy in business process terms facilitates both implementation and communication. Frequently, the thrust of corporate strategy involves some mix of introducing new products or services, improving service to customers, and reducing cost. Most organizations find that business process thinking helps articulate these initiatives in plain language, with measurable results. Granted, there are certain aspects of strategy such as product pricing and brand positioning where business process context may not add much. Yet, in the vast majority of cases, strategy is best expressed, as Porter emphasized in his 1996 HBR article, in terms of the choice of activities and how they are performed. The key steps involved here include assessing the gap between current and desired performance in business process terms, and developing a business process management plan that clearly indicates the ownership of the enterprise-level business processes and the degree of improvement for each business process. A couple of the major pitfalls in these steps include failing to achieve consensus on key priorities and planning to do too much too fast."

3) The third principle is to articulate the firm's strategy such that it *inspires,* from the boardroom to the lunchroom, and remains front and center throughout the year. This third principle rounds out the cluster of three key principles related to what I call Strategic Focus. Why do this? Implementing strategy requires that people be on the same page in terms of what needs to be done. This involves linking vision and mission to key strategic initiatives expressed in business process terms, such that people can relate their individual efforts in making strategy happen. The main output of these activities is a communication plan. The major pitfalls include the excessive use of jargon and buzzwords, failing to have a consistent message across groups, and not cascading the key messages to the front line."

4) The fourth principle has been positioned as the launching pad for organizational alignment. It states that action needs to be taken to assure that the organization's core business processes are designed to deliver on its strategic goals. Again, work gets done via business processes. The key steps include a mid-level analysis to flesh out and validate the scope of work indicated by the business process management plan. The Process Owner role is crucial in this respect, as cross-process issues are identified and resolved. And the primary pitfalls to avoid include not making the investment in relevant and effective business process training for middle management, failing to maintain momentum, and not installing the infrastructure for the regular dialogue between the business process management teams and senior management, including the Board of Directors."

5) "The fifth principle says that the organization design must enable business process execution. In this context,

organization design is defined as the composite of structure, measures and rewards. Putting this into practice relies upon mid-level business process analysis and is often an iterative method linked to business process improvement activities. We've already discussed that there's a lot to avoid here. I'll just mention the key pitfall, which is jumping prematurely from strategy to structure and failing to adequately reflect on the central role of business processes."

6) "The sixth key principle addresses the need to assess and deploy enabling technology based on the value added through enhanced business process performance. Why? Business process performance relies increasingly on enabling technology and process automation. Again it takes iterative work to put this principle into action. Also, as we just discussed this morning it requires that the senior team take accountability for IT investments. As the leadership team develops an understanding of the performance and the key gaps in the execution of key business processes, they should acquire a very clear sense of where technology will enable performance and can make more informed decisions on which IT projects should be funded, what results can be expected, and what the likely payback might be. Again, we've already discussed several of the pitfalls, so I'll just mention the major one, which in my view, is the reluctance of the senior team to step up to the bar on technology issues and take the easy way out by delegating to the CIO decisions the business leadership should take."

7) "The seventh principle states that it's essential to hard wire the enterprise-wide performance measurement system to budgets and operating reviews. The potential for BPM systems to automatically "build-in" business process meas-

ures is essential in this regard. We are all creatures of habit, and the repeated and regular review of business process performance via operating reviews is necessary to fully install this mode of thinking. However, this is a big change for most companies, and as with most change, there will be some friction. So leaders need to be ready for it. This is so important that I stated it as a separate principle, although it could be argued that it's a subset of the eighth principle. The major pitfall here is simply failing to do it, or maintain it."

8) "Which brings us to the eighth and final principle of sustaining focus and alignment. This is where the rubber really hits the road – where leadership resolve is tested with respect to having the courage and determination to make the necessary investments in people and technology. The key pitfall here is failing to stick to the critical initiatives, sending mixed messages, and forgetting to communicate persistently."

"Why do I use the term 'sustain?' Simply because enterprise process management is a journey. It's not a sprint. Along the way we've got to be ready for a lot of good, bad and even ugly surprises. Again, the degree of success to be realized in these key activities is driven by Process Owners and the success factors include:

- finding multiple ways, using multiple media to communicate strategy,
- developing the framework to link measures and rewards to operating practices,
- introducing a set of visible and considerable recognition and rewards for those who significantly improve the company's ability to deliver on customer needs, and

• embracing continuous change and innovation by continually investing in people and enabling technology."

"So, that's the recap. We have time for one or two questions before we move on to the case study. Questions, anyone?"

***

"I have a couple of questions, but let's start with complacency," Fred said. "What does one do when some members of the executive team think that things are just fine? They say – sure, we're making less money than before, but we're still profitable and that's a lot better than some companies out there."

"That's a tough one – and unfortunately – far too common," Peter said. "I suspect that Polaroid might not be in Chapter 11 if their leadership team had recognized the threat from digital cameras earlier. I think Kotter provides some excellent guidance in his article, *Leading Change.* It's essential to create a climate of urgency, and in this regard I've observed that if the executive are not fired up by the gap between current and desired performance, it's sometimes constructive to leverage a real or anticipated external threat as a means to crack the wall of complacency. This could be a competitive threat, an evolving technology or even anticipated government regulation."

Fred said, "Uh-huh, we could probably do something around competitive threats or government regulation."

Peter picked up on the latter point, "You wouldn't be alone. Recent financial reporting scandals have already generated new government regulations. Right now, there is much talk in companies about how they comply with the Sarbanes-Oxley Act that mandates clear internal controls around financial reporting and its governance. To comply, companies have a choice of deploying appropriate business process automation, or throwing huge quantities of human resources at the problem. The experience gained from taking on this government mandate could be one more catalyst for reinvigorating business process thinking – and action – in any company."

"In any case," Peter continued, "you can figure out what might be the best approach to deal with complacency. But my experience is that organizations are reluctant to change existing management practices unless three conditions are met. There needs to be a certain level of real or perceived *pain*, a clear *gap* between current and desired performance and a deep management *commitment* to do things differently. In the absence of these three conditions, it's a tough row to hoe. I mean you just can't say to the leadership team that it should implement business process management. That's like saying 'take your medicine, it's good for you.' Do you see what I mean?"

"Yes, that's helpful," Fred said. "Also, it brings me to the next question. It's clear to me, that business process thinking is intrinsic to managing organizational capability. But a number of our colleagues only understand business process at a low level. They basically see it as 'a bunch of procedures' and not true cross-functional, enterprise business processes. What can be done about that?"

"That's a bit easier to address than the complacency issue, simply because there's a clear element of knowledge and skill. That's a gap that can be closed with education and training," Peter explained. "Nevertheless, the training must be relevant and people have to have an open mind for the education and training to work. Recently, I've been leaning toward using company specific business process examples to increase relevance to reduce the length of training per day, especially for middle managers, from eight hours to six hours so people can address their urgent daily tasks. All right, we have time for just one more question."

Jim asked, "Is there a profile for a company that can best take advantage of enterprise process management? I mean, is it more suitable for some companies than others?"

"That's hard to say," Peter replied. "In theory, business process management can work for any organization. In practice, and this is just based on my experience, I'd have to say that BPM is best suited for moderately successful companies who have greater aspirations. When leaders chose to implement BPM, they find that it energizes the organization and provides context for several of the essential leadership behaviors outlined by Bossidy and Charan in the summary you read last night. Effectively implemented, BPM can help good companies become great companies. Does that answer your question?"

Jim nodded.

***

"Fine," Peter said, as he started to hand out the case materials. "Then let's proceed to this course's major case exercise. It's based on REMOCO, the regional mortgage company we briefly discussed a couple of days ago. This case will provide you with the means to integrate and apply the eight essential principles of business process management in a hypothetical and risk-free setting. There are three clearly marked, sealed envelopes I'm handing out. Please open them in sequence as outlined in your case instructions.

This case will provide you with the experience of applying the eight principles. It will take you close to three hours to complete, and as I mentioned, I've arranged for lunch to be provided. Any questions?"

There were none.

"Then, let's split into two teams to work on the case. I'd suggest Dave's side of the table go down to our break-out room —that's room number 102, as we did yesterday, and Fred's side of the table stay here."

***

It did take until the middle of the afternoon for the two teams to work out their solutions to the case, present their results to one another and discuss their findings. There were a few final questions that Peter addressed.

Then he referred back to the participants' expectations that were still posted on the flipchart from the initial introductions and asked the participants to comment on the degree to which these had been met.

Once this was done, he said, "We're at the home stretch. Let me express my thanks to you right now for your participation in the workshop. I sincerely hope you've found these concepts to be worthwhile. In the time that remains, I'd encourage you to develop your personal action plan. Please feel free to work individually or in small groups as you may wish. Also, I'll be here for another hour to answer any special, company-specific questions you may have. I'd also ask you to complete the course feedback forms that I passed out earlier. Thanks again. You've been a great group."

The participants recognized White's effort with an enthusiastic round of applause. As people began to work, Peter turned to gather up his materials.

***

A few minutes later, Lori went over to where Peter was sitting and handed him the course feedback form. She shook his hand and said, "I just wanted to thank you. The program really opened my eyes on several fronts. To be candid, though, I don't think our company is ready for this approach quite yet. In my opinion, it's just too much change for us, and there's too much going on right now with three major product launches being planned for the next six months."

"That's fine, Lori" Peter said. "I'm pleased you found some value, and I enjoyed your participation. But let me leave you with an observation or two. If I recall correctly, the average life expectancy of a publicly held company used to be over 50 years, but today it's around 10 and dropping. That means that your comment, 'it's just too much change for us,' will be no defense against the reality and cruelty of the marketplace. Companies that are heads-down in doing what they are currently doing – extrapolating past success, doing more of the same – had better lift their eyes to the economic horizon from time to time, or become a footnote in business history. All too often, the mindset that made today's business leaders successful is the same mindset that blinds them to change. They sometimes get stuck in that box; mistakenly thinking that what worked for them in the past will guarantee the future."

"So, I'd challenge you to use what you've learned, become a change agent in your company and ignite your team to think out of the box. If that doesn't work, send me your resume when your company finally gets gobbled up by the change monster that is prowling every industry. I'll be happy to help you find a position in a company that embraces, rather than cringes at change, for they will still be around."

"Challenge accepted," Lori said. "Don't be surprised to see my boss, our VP of Sales, in your next session."

Peter returned to sorting his materials. Over the next little while, a number of the participants sought him out to discuss some aspect of their individual action plan.

Eventually, people began to disperse. Peter exchanged warm farewells with Bob and Glen.

Soon Peter was the only one left in the meeting room. He soaked in the silence and reflected on the past three days. He pondered which of the participants would act as catalysts for business process management in their own organizations. He smiled to himself as thought of yet another Yogism, "when you come to a fork in the road – take it." That's exactly what these executives will be facing.

"Which ones would take action and become the new champions in their industries?" he asked himself. "Time would tell, and yet there simply isn't a lot of time left for some organizations. Those who fail to transform the traditional functional mindset and embrace business process thinking will find themselves teetering on the brink. Indeed, BPM is a highly competitive team sport, and in the playoffs for industry championships, it's win or be eliminated."

Resources

These resources are available for viewing or purchase at www.anclote.com/spanyi.html

Bensaou, M. and Michael Earl, "The Right Mind-Set for Managing Information Technology," *Harvard Business Review*, September-October 1998, pgs 118-128

Brache, Alan, *How Organizations Work*, Wiley, 2002.

Bossidy, Larry and Ram Charan, *Execution: The Discipline of Getting Things Done*, Crown Business, 2002.

Davenport, Thomas H., "Putting the Enterprise into the Enterprise System," *Harvard Business Review*, July - August 1998, pgs 121-131.

Drucker, Peter, *Management Challenges of the 21st Century*, Harper Business, 1999.

Eisenhardt, Kathleen M. and Donald N. Sull, "Strategy as Simple Rules," *Harvard Business Review*, January, 2001, pgs 106-116.

Fingar, Peter, "The Real-Time Enterprise," *Internet World*, June, 2001.

Galbraith, Jay, *Designing Organizations*, Jossey-Bass, 1995.

Gould, Michael and Andrew Campbell, "Do you have a Well-Designed Organization?" *Harvard Business Review*, March 2002, pgs 117-124.

Hagel III, John and John Seely Brown, "Your Next IT Strategy," *Harvard Business Review,* October 2001, pgs 105-113.

Hamel, Gary, *Leading the Revolution,* Harvard Business School Press, 2000.

Hamel, Gary, "Strategy as Revolution," *Harvard Business Review,* July-August 1996, pgs 69-82.

Hammer, Michael, "Process Management and the Future of Six Sigma," *Sloan Management Review,* Winter 2002, pgs 26-32.

Hammer, Michael, "The Superefficient Company," *Harvard Business Review,* September 2001, pgs 82-91.

Hammer, Michael and Steven Stanton, "How Process Enterprises Really Work," *Harvard Business Review,* November - December 1999, pgs 108-118.

Kaplan, Robert S. and David P. Norton, "Having Trouble with Your Strategy? Then Map It," *Harvard Business Review,* September-October 2000, pgs 167-176.

Kaplan, Robert S. and David P. Norton, *The Strategy-Focused Organization,* Harvard Business School Press, 2001.

Kaplan, Robert S. and David P. Norton, "Using the Balanced Scorecard as a Strategic Management System," *Harvard Business Review,* January- February 1996, pgs 75-85.

Kotter, John, "What Leaders Really Do," *Harvard Business Review,* Special Issue December 2001.

Kotter, John, "Leading Change: Why Transformation Efforts Fail," *Harvard Business Review.* March-April 1995, pgs 59-67.

Majchrak, Ann and Qianwei Wang, "Breaking the Functional Mindset in Process Organizations," *Harvard Business Review,* September - October 1996, pgs 92-99.

Mintzberg, Henry and Joseph Lampel, "Reflecting on the Strategy Process," *Sloan Management Review,* Spring 1999, pgs 21-30.

Nadler, David A., and Michael L. Tushman, *Competing by Design,* Oxford University Press, 1997.

Porter, Michael, "What is Strategy?" *Harvard Business Review,* November-December 1996, pgs 61-78.

Porter, Michael, "Strategy and the Internet," *Harvard Business Review,* March 2001, pgs 62-78.

Rodin, Robert, *Free, Perfect, and Now,* Simon & Schuster, 1999.

Ross, Jeanne W. and Peter Weill, "Six IT Decisions Your IT People Shouldn't Make," *Harvard Business Review,* November 2002, pgs 84-91.

Rummler, Geary A. and Alan Brache, *Improving Performance: How to Manage the White Space on the Organization Chart,* Jossey-Bass, 1995.

Smith, Howard and Peter Fingar, *Business Process Management: The Third Wave,* Meghan-Kiffer Press, 2003.

Smith, Howard and Peter Fingar, "The Humble Yet Mighty Business Process, *Darwin Magazine,* February 2003.

Smith, Howard, "Making Business Processes Manageable," *Web-Services Journal,* June 2002.

Smith, Howard and Peter Fingar, "Business Processes: From Modeling to Management" and "BPM's Third Wave: Build To Adapt, Not Just To Last," *eBizQ Online,* 2003.

Treacy, Michael and Fred Wiersema, *The Discipline of Market Leaders,* Addison Wesley, 1995.

Yogi Berra quotes can be found at links on www.anclote.com/spanyi.html

References

[1] Davenport, Thomas H., *Process Innovation: Reengineering Work through Information Technology,* Harvard Business School Press, 1993.
[2] William Oncken. *The Impact of Communications on Productivity.* The William Oncken Company, 1954.
[3] Drucker, Peter F., *Management Challenges of the 21st Century,* HarperBusiness, 1999.

About the Author

Andrew Spanyi is the Managing Director of Spanyi International Inc., a consulting and training company that operates in the field of organization and business process design.

Spanyi was previously affiliated with the well-known business process innovation firm, The Rummler-Brache Group [RBG], as a Principal of the firm, and subsequently as Managing Partner of the Canadian practice. In these roles, Andrew managed or participated in over 100 major performance improvement projects across several key industries in both the USA and Canada.

He served as the Senior Vice President of SCONA, a specialty financial services firm, with responsibility for new product introduction and geographic expansion. He was the Director of Marketing and Product Development for the Canadian division of Xerox Learning Systems (a.k.a. Learning International, Achieve Global) and significantly increased the volume and quality of custom training programs in the areas of management and sales skill development.

Spanyi is regularly asked to speak at conferences on business process management, and has written extensively on business process issues in publications, including Industrial Engineer Magazine, Contingency Planning & Management, Wireless Review and Plant Magazine.

He earned an MBA [Marketing/Finance] from York University, Toronto, Ontario, Canada, and is a member of the American Management Association and the American Society for Quality. He can be reached at andrew@spanyi.com.

Bring Your Team Up To Speed . . .

Business Process Management is a Team Sport $29.95

Let your colleagues know they can obtain the litle BIG book of business process thinking at
www.anclote.com/order.html

Order multiple copies for your entire team and enjoy significant discounts on this game-changing book.

Substantial discounts are available to work groups and major discounts are available for corporate-wide purchases.

For details, visit
www.anclote.com/order.html
or send us email at
volumeOrders@anclote.com

Advanced Business-Technology Books from Meghan-Kiffer Press

Business Process Management:
The Third Wave
Harvard Business School's *Working Knowledge*
Featured Book Recommendation

The Death of 'e' and the Birth of the
Real New Economy:
Business Models, Technologies and Strategies
for the 21st Century
Internet World Magazine
Must Read Book of the Year

Enterprise E-Commerce
The Breakthrough for Business-to-Business Commerce

The Real-Time Enterprise
Powering Profits with Process Automation

Meghan-Kiffer Press
Tampa, Florida, USA
www.mkpress.com
Advanced Business-Technology Books for Competitive Advantage